100 GREATEST CYCLING CLIMBS

OF THE

TOUR DE FRANCE

A CYCLIST'S GUIDE TO RIDING THE MOUNTAINS OF THE TOUR

SIMON WARREN

F

FRANCES
LINCOLN

100 Greatest Cycling Climbs of the Tour de France:
A Cyclist's Guide to Riding the Mountains of the Tour
© 2014 Quarto Publishing plc.
Text, photographs, design and illustrations © Simon Warren 2014

First Published in 2017 by Frances Lincoln,
an imprint of The Quarto Group.
The Old Brewery, 6 Blundell Street,
London N7 9BH, United Kingdom.
www.QuartoKnows.com

A catalogue record for this book is available from the British Library.

978-0-7112-3482-6

Printed and bound in China

3 4 5 6 7 8 9

Brimming with creative inspiration, how-to projects and useful information to enrich
your everyday life, Quarto Knows is a favourite destination for those pursuing their
interests and passions. Visit our site and dig deeper with our books into your area of
interest: Quarto Creates, Quarto Cooks, Quarto Homes, Quarto Lives, Quarto Drives,
Quarto Explores, Quarto Gifts, or Quarto Kids.

FOR CHAR, LUX, AND RYDER

Contents

5

Prelude

The Tour de France was conceived in 1903 when, according to legend, the struggling newspaper *L'Auto* was looking for a promotional vehicle to boost its sales and ultimately to put its rival *Le Vélo* out of business. Its creation is popularly attributed to Henri Desgrange but the idea, the spark – that came from a young journalist, Géo Lefèvre. His suggestion of a six day race around the whole of France was jumped upon by the editor Desgrange and with the paper's accountant, Victor Goddet, keen to bankroll the affair, the Tour de France was born. Back in those early years the riders covered stage distances that would make Audax riders wince, over roads unfit for 4x4 vehicles on bikes you wouldn't salvage from a skip. The first race was won by Maurice Garin who covered the 2,428 kilometres at an average speed of 25.68km/h which is quite pedestrian compared with the current average speeds that are just shy of 40km/h.

Over the years, the format of the route, the formation of teams, and the distances covered were in constant flux as the race sought the perfect solution. It wasn't until 1919 that the first iconic yellow jersey, the ubiquitous symbol of the Tour, was awarded and not until 1969 that the race settled into the format we are all familiar with today. Later still, in 1975, the polka dot jersey was introduced. Fought for on the roads in this book, it is awarded to the rider with the most points in the mountain classification. A system was devised to categorize each climb relating to the car gear required to drive up its slope; a 4th category could be crossed in 4th gear and so on. The lower the number the more points are awarded up to the *Hors Catégorie*: roads so hard they're beyond classification.

The first 'mountain', a road over 1,000m to be crossed by the Tour was the Col de la République (see page 92), in the inaugural race in 1903. Having coped with that challenge, two years later it was time to test the riders on a real climb, the Ballon d'Alsace (see page 122), up to a height of 1,178m. Desgrange saw the climb as more of an experiment and stated that no one would be able to ride over it, but one man, René Pottier, proved him wrong.

The real watershed moment arrived in 1910 when the race was sent over the high passes of the Pyrenees, starting with the Col de Peyresourde (see page 40) and finishing four mountains later in Bayonne after crossing the Col d'Aubisque (see page 24). It all but destroyed the riders but it made the race, and it was on that day that the Tour really began. There was no looking back; the next year the Alps were introduced with an ascent of the Col du Galibier and anyone who wanted to win the Tour had to learn – A to climb, and B to descend these formidable roads.

Living the dream

What a summer, what an amazing summer, it was the chance of a lifetime; the task, to ride and document 100 mountains from the Pyrenees to the Vosges to compile the book you hold in your hand. I'd written books on the 'tiny' hills of Britain and Belgium, but this was a whole different ball game – these roads were colossal by comparison. You could argue that the book should have just been called *The Greatest Cycling Climbs of France*, but would they be household names if it wasn't for the race? The Tour was, is, and forever will be the world's greatest sporting event and these roads are its building blocks, its beating heart. To ride these climbs is to ride in the shadows of giants, to add your tyre tracks to those of the hundreds of battles that have taken place on the very same slopes. Some higher, some steeper, many famous and some seemingly insignificant, but all are essential in creating the legend that is the Tour.

On top of my very first mountain, I'm in the white cricket hat and yes, denim look Lycra!

To be expected, choosing the climbs wasn't easy as the race has crossed a vast amount of cols over its hundred-year history and at times tough choices had to be made. In listing them all, from the Joux Plane to Luz-Ardiden, my mouth watered with the prospect ahead, but my legs trembled; it was going to take some effort. So, with the 100 written down I headed off to Stanfords in Covent Garden to bulk-buy Michelin maps and started planning the trips.

This wouldn't be the first time I'd taken a bike to the mountains – that was back in 1992 when I joined a coach trip following the Tour for a week. After a couple of brief glimpses of the race we arrived at the base of the Col du Télégraph and it was time to get our bikes out. This was to be my very first mountain, and I couldn't wait. We jumped out of the bus, clipped in, and set off, and to this day I will never forget that ride. The views over the valley every time the trees broke, the gain in altitude – I was so happy I was almost laughing out loud. That night we stayed in Valoire where we all had a few too many beers, especially considering none of us drank much either side of Christmas, and this was going to make the next day's ascent of the Galibier a whole lot harder.

Five metres in and I'd been dropped, I had the hangover from hell and it looked as if I was going to be in for a very long day. 'Go ahead' I shouted, 'Leave me', as our group disappeared into the distance abandoning me to wallow in self-pity. But wait, I was on the Col du Galibier, I couldn't go down like this, so I pulled myself together and slowly started to pick up speed. By the halfway point I had riders in my sights. Round the bend, on to the steeper slopes, one by one I began to pick them off, and then with 5 kilometres to go I'd caught and dropped the last of our group. In my element, I pushed to the summit as hard as I could to finish the climb battling elbow-to-elbow with a giant Belgian in a sprint for the line. What a mountain, what an experience – this is what the bike was invented for.

So, back to 2013, with my maps laid out and calendar in hand, I started to plan. I worked out that I had thirty days to ride all 100 climbs and would split the research into five trips built around the school and bank holidays. On paper the plan looked faultless, but I was soon to realize that the window for mountain climbing wasn't quite as wide as I'd hoped.

Tired at the top of the Tourmalet and triumphant on the Col de Pailheres, both over 2000 metres

The first expedition was pencilled in for the end of May: ten days in the Pyrenees riding west to east. The research I'd done predicted the roads would be well clear of snow by then, but unfortunately it didn't forecast the winter of 2012–2013. A week prior to my departure the top of the Col du Tourmalet was still covered in 2m of snow; I had to reschedule. Postponing the trip for a month, I felt sure I would be fine, but fate was to deal the project another blow when, days before I was due to leave, all that snow melted practically overnight washing not only the roads but whole villages right off the mountains. Frustrated and approaching the halfway point of the year, I ditched the Pyrenees and decided to head first to the Jura and Vosges ranges.

The first climb was to be the Col du Grand Colombier. Following the drive south from Calais I climbed out of the car, and an hour later it was one down, ninety-nine to

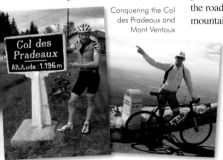

Conquering the Col des Pradeaux and Mont Ventoux

go! That first trip was by far the most hectic, and I'm frequently reminded by my wife that it was at times 'a living nightmare'. I didn't see the problem of eating cold pizza at 10 at night while driving round twisted roads with a one-year-old boy screaming in the back – it's all part of the adventure, right? Apparently not.

For the next trip I left the family, the travel cot, and the masses of luggage and instead travelled light with my mate Owen. This was a laid-back trip: five days following that year's race around the Alps. We bagged the necessary cols but we also had three wonderful afternoons sitting on mountains, soaking in the race atmosphere while gorging on fine cheese, fresh bread, and saucisson.

Trip three and it was back to the Alps, and back with the family in tow. I promised it'd be less stressful this time and also promised four days by the pool halfway through, on our journey from Geneva to Nice and back. The further south we travelled, the more amazing the scenery became. I was blown away by the grandeur, the emptiness, the magnificence of the Southern Alps – even my daughter looked out of the car window at times to take in the views, and that is really saying something.

A week after returning from sixteen days of glorious climbing, I was on the road again with my next travelling partner, Nick. We raced around the Massif Central, doing up to five climbs a day so we could reach Mont Ventoux with enough time to really enjoy it. And

Thumbs up from the Port de Bales and a fantastic welcome at the summit of the Col de Vars

that we did, riding the fantastic loop from Malaucène, via Bédoin, over the climb, and back to tuck into a gorgeous pizza – it was the best day's riding of the whole summer. It had all been very relaxed, but we did have one more climb to ride, and looking at the time I realized we would have to get a move on. What followed was an atrocious four-hour drive to Mende, arriving just before we lost the light, then another three-hour slog up the motorway to reach our hotel just two minutes before the door was bolted.

The final trip was the twice-postponed journey to the Pyrenees, and for this one my dad volunteered to be co-pilot so long as I let him go birdwatching at the top of each mountain. It turned out to be the perfect arrangement: we would drive to the top of a col, I'd leave dad there to wander off looking for lammergeiers as I rode down then up, before we moved on. We repeated this four to five times a day then ate like kings each evening. It was without a doubt the best cycling trip

I'd ever been on, Dad even did all the in between climbs driving. I was, quite simply, living the dream.

The summer wasn't an endless bed of roses – one filled with breakfasts, lunches, and dinners on the move. There were times when I questioned my sanity and had to remind myself that I was having the time of my life.

Two low points come to mind right away, the first being my ascent of the Col du Glandon. While unpacking the bike at the base, there was a little moisture in the air, but also chinks of blue sky. I was optimistic. The further I rode, though, the worse the conditions became; light rain turned to hard rain, and then I heard thunder, then – FLASH – lightning illuminated the very cloud I was riding through. My heart pounded. I had to get to the top, but I really wasn't having fun; in fact I'd rather have been anywhere else. Determined to reach the summit I pressed on, but with three bends and just 750m to go I chickened out. Shivering by the roadside, cowering from the violent sky, I did my best to take the pictures I needed before pulling on my sodden jacket to begin the most

hideous of descents back down a river of a road to the car.

My worst moment, however, was on the ride up to Superbagnères. With five days in the Pyrenees and twenty mountains in my legs I hit the wall, cracked, I lost my legs and my head. As there were no kilometre markers on the climb, I'd forgotten how far it was to go and was riding through thick, low cloud. I had to reach the summit as my dad was waiting up there with the car, but where was the summit? Those final kilometres lasted forever; revolution by revolution, I just crawled upwards, wishing it to end. Finally the giant hotel that sits at the top appeared; the end was in sight. I rolled over the brow, and then head back to the car where I climbed off the bike to just lie curled up on the ground, a broken man. Next day, though, after plenty of food and a good sleep I had one of my best days of the whole adventure – I'd gone through a world of suffering to come out the other side reborn!

As for the highlights, it would be impossible to list those – there were quite literally hundreds of them, from my crack-of-dawn raid on the Cine de la Bonnette, to tackling the wickedly steep slopes of the Pas du Payrol. From the cows ringing their bells supporting me up the Col de Soulour, to the joy of finishing the last climb at the top of Arcalis. I was truly blessed to have had this wonderful opportunity, France is a beautiful country and riding in the mountains is the very best way to explore it.

Lying broken at the top of Superbagnères

The Marmotte

You're on the sofa at home watching the Tour on TV, 'Come on' you shout, 'Attack! What are you waiting for?' It looks easy on TV doesn't it? But have you ever ridden 175 kilometres across four mountain passes? At race pace? Well, before you chastise your idols any further you need to try it for yourself. Of course I don't mean ride the Tour, but to ride an event that will give you, the mortal, an experience of being a Tour rider for a day: The Marmotte.

Named after that most elusive of Alpine mammals, The Marmotte, originally run in 1982, is widely acknowledged as the world's first, and to this day, toughest single-day cyclosportive. Events come and go, all claiming to be the biggest and baddest, but The Marmotte is the standard they are all judged by. Leaving Bourg-d'Oisans you embark on a giant loop taking in the cols du Glandon, Télégraphe, and Galibier before finishing at the top of Alpe d'Huez. In one punishing day you will cover 175 kilometres and climb a massive 5,180m.

The day begins in the cold mountain shadows, as you line up patiently but nervously, waiting to start. The Marmotte isn't a race; if it were, riders would amble away from town. No, The Marmotte is far more serious, which is why riders leave the start as if fired from a cannon. All the way to the base of the Col du Glandon it's hell for leather as everyone fights for wheels, jumping from train to train along the valley floor. It's imperative that you NEVER push too hard here but equally important that you cover the ground as quickly as possible. So ride smart, ride economically, suck the wheels, and look for that armchair ride that will take you to the base of the first climb. Alliances made on the flat, though, will splinter as soon as you hit the slopes of this staggering 24-kilometre climb. Take it steady, ride within yourself, ride at YOUR pace no matter what those around you are doing. It's

THE START IS FRANTIC, KEEP YOUR WITS ABOUT YOU, FOLLOW WHEELS BUT NEVER GO TOO HARD, STAY FRESH

TAKE CARE DOWN THIS STEEP DESCENT AS IT COULD EASILY END YOUR RIDE IF YOU OVERCOOK A SHARP BEND

STAY SHELTERED, RIDE IN A LARGE GROUP AND MORE IMPORTANTLY EAT, EAT, EAT, AND DRINK , DRINK, DRINK

BOURG-D'OISANS

LE RIVIER

COL DU GLANDON 1924m

easy to get carried away by the euphoria of riding these magical mountains with thousands of like-minded souls – just keep a lid on it.

Down the dangerous descent you arrive at the long valley floor that leads to the Col du Télégraphe. Here the key, as at the start, is to stay in the wheels. Be alert, watch for splits as the groups contract and expand like giant organisms; stay with those willing to push the pace but only, ONLY work, if it's an absolute necessity. Once on the Télégraphe you can open the tanks that little bit more; you'll be well warmed up and hopefully fatigue won't have kicked in yet. Over the top and there's a short descent into Valoire. Shake your legs, stretch, and drink your bottles dry, ready to be refilled. Through the feed stop and it's on to the mighty Galibier, it's this giant climb that will make or break your day. Try again to measure your effort, but by now your legs will be hurting and all pedalling will soon be tough. I have a rule that I never use my smallest sprocket until I reach the

bend at the halfway point, as it's here that things turn really nasty. If you reach the summit with something still in your legs then you should be on a good ride; if you've already blown, then the rest of your day will take you to new levels of suffering. The next 50 kilometres are almost entirely downhill but packed with perilous tunnels that turn day to night in an instant and a handful of steep ramps that are such a shock to the system that they will bring tears to the eyes.

Once back on the valley floor you line up for Alpe d'Huez – just one more climb, 13 kilometres between you and the finish. You must refuel before you hit its vicious slopes which, right from the base, will be littered with exhausted riders, their bodies broken, their minds lost. By now each pedal revolution will be agony, and I swear, with four kilometres to go you'll be screaming that you will NEVER, I SAY NEVER, EVER ride a bike again. Around you, competitors will be pushing their machines, dragging them even, limping to the summit, but none will give up because this is The Marmotte, the greatest single day on a bike an amateur can have.

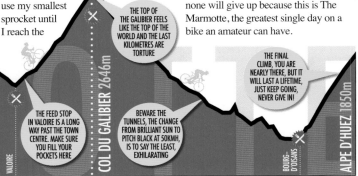

THE TOP OF THE GALIBIER FEELS LIKE THE TOP OF THE WORLD AND THE LAST KILOMETRES ARE TORTURE

THE FINAL CLIMB, YOU ARE NEARLY THERE, BUT IT WILL LAST A LIFETIME, JUST KEEP GOING, NEVER GIVE IN!

THE FEED STOP IN VALOIRE IS A LONG WAY PAST THE TOWN CENTRE. MAKE SURE YOU FILL YOUR POCKETS HERE

BEWARE THE TUNNELS, THE CHANGE FROM BRILLIANT SUN TO PITCH BLACK AT 50KMH, IS TO SAY THE LEAST, EXHILARATING

VALOIRE

COL DU GALIBIER 2646m

BOURG-D'OISANS

ALPE D'HUEZ 1850m

Instructions

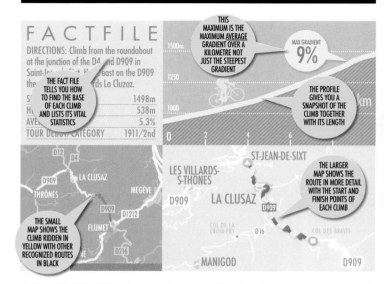

FACTFILE

DIRECTIONS: Climb from the roundabout at the junction of the D4 and D909 in Saint-Jean-de-Sixt. Head east on the D909 the ... towards La Cluzaz.

THE FACT FILE TELLS YOU HOW TO FIND THE BASE OF EACH CLIMB AND LISTS ITS VITAL STATISTICS

S...	1498m
H...	538m
AVE...	5.3%
TOUR DEBUT CATEGORY	1911/2nd

THIS MAXIMUM IS THE MAXIMUM AVERAGE GRADIENT OVER A KILOMETRE NOT JUST THE STEEPEST GRADIENT

MAX GRADIENT
9%

THE PROFILE GIVES YOU A SNAPSHOT OF THE CLIMB TOGETHER WITH ITS LENGTH

THE LARGER MAP SHOWS THE ROUTE IN MORE DETAIL WITH THE START AND FINISH POINTS OF EACH CLIMB

THE SMALL MAP SHOWS THE CLIMB RIDDEN IN YELLOW WITH OTHER RECOGNIZED ROUTES IN BLACK

LOCATIONS

On each page you will find two maps, one showing the area the climb sits in and another that pinpoints the exact route. Although you should be able to locate each hill using these I would always recommend you take a comprehensive map of the area or a GPS/satnav device to cross-reference.

RATINGS

The climbs are rated within the context of the book. The rating is an amalgamation of gradient, length, the likely hostility of the riding conditions and the condition of the surface. All the climbs are tough, therefore 1/10 equals 'hard', and 10/10 equals almost impossible.

KEY TO THE MAPS

Motorway	**A43**
D Road	**D1006**
Minor Road	SUMMIT ★ D78
Climb	ROUTE USED ●——— ALTERNATE ROUTE
Climb	START FINISH
Border	FRANCE / ITALY
Town	**TOWN** ⌐ SMALLER TOWN
Scale	10km

!

WARNING

One last thing before
we get started: while it
may be 30 degrees in the
valley, that doesn't mean it
won't be snowing at the top. So always,
ALWAYS take a jacket. Now, to the Mountains!

PYRE

AQUITAINE

MI

PAU

TARBES

OLORON

LOURDES

LANNEMEZ

③

①

⑤

②

④

⑥

⑨

⑬

⑦

⑧

⑩

⑪

⑫

SPAIN

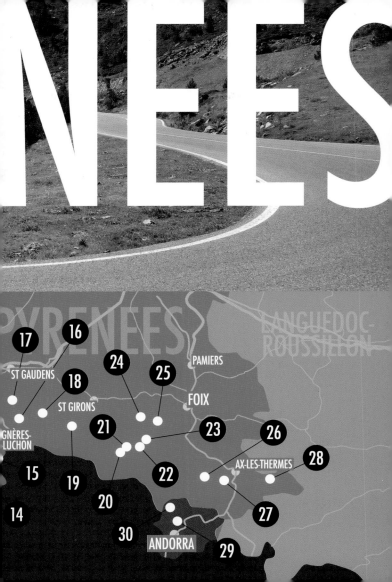

1 Port de Larrau

The Port de Larrau was my very first Pyrenean climb. I'd heard the old wives' tales, 'Oh, the Pyrenees, they may be shorter than the Alps, but they're much harder, much harder'. Could they be that much harder? Really? Starting from the Auburge Logibar, the road rises steeply straight away towards Larrau; pass through the small town, exit, and it's time to test the claims. The next 3 kilometres are relentless, every last metre of them set on a 10% slope – it has all come true – welcome to the Pyrenees! At the 4-kilometre mark you are afforded the briefest of rests, and then it's back to climbing on the 10% gradient that never gives in, not for a moment. The difference between a climb that averages 7% and one that averages 9% may look slight on paper, but in reality it's a quantum leap – you're not in Kansas anymore. A viciously hard ramp takes you up to a mini summit where, admittedly, 11 kilometres in, you can relax for a while before continuing on a gentle slope, dodging the lethargic cattle scattered over the road. After this, you've a chunk more climbing before you reach the end: wind through a set of hairpins beneath jagged peaks to finish, overwhelmed, at the small plateau and the border with Spain.

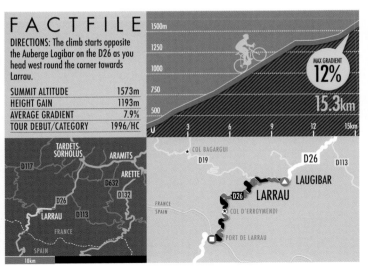

FACTFILE

DIRECTIONS: The climb starts opposite the Auberge Logibar on the D26 as you head west round the corner towards Larrau.

SUMMIT ALTITUDE	1573m
HEIGHT GAIN	1193m
AVERAGE GRADIENT	7.9%
TOUR DEBUT/CATEGORY	1996/HC

MAX GRADIENT **12%**

15.3km

1500m · 1250 · 1000 · 750 · 500

0 3 6 9 12 15km

TARDETS-SORHOLUS
ARAMITS
ARETTE
D117
D632
D132
D26
LARRAU
D113
FRANCE
SPAIN
10km

COL BAGARGUI
D19
D26
D113
LAUGIBAR
LARRAU
FRANCE
SPAIN
COL D'ERROYMENDI
PORT DE LARRAU

2 Col du Soudet

The climb starts in Arette, but as the entirety of the first 7 kilometres are set on a 2% slope, I ignored them and began my ascent at La Mouline. I'd had my baptism of fire earlier in the day on the Port du Larrau but still wasn't convinced that all the Pyrenean climbs would be that hard – but once I'd finished this one I was. Leaving La Mouline, it's not long before you pass signs advertising 15% gradient: great, bring it on! You keep riding, looking round the bends in anticipation but there's nothing, and then just as I began to think I'd been mis-sold some of the steep stuff, it arrives to stop me dead. Once you've dragged yourself through a very testing 100m it's time to get stuck into the meat of the climb – shifting between 9 and 11% it wears you down, chips away at your resources, your willpower. Take a look on the map and you will see the Col de Soudet isn't in fact the only peak of the road, and heading in this direction there are three recognized cols to cross, but with no subsequent descents they are merely small brows, points to aim for, set in the achingly beautiful landscape. The summit, which again isn't actually the summit, arrives at the junction with the D113, but the road continues upwards to peak at the Pas d'Arlas.

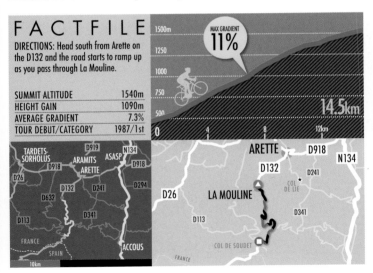

FACTFILE

DIRECTIONS: Head south from Arette on the D132 and the road starts to ramp up as you pass through La Mouline.

SUMMIT ALTITUDE	1540m
HEIGHT GAIN	1090m
AVERAGE GRADIENT	7.3%
TOUR DEBUT/CATEGORY	1987/1st

MAX GRADIENT
11%

14.5km

3 Col de Marie-Blanque

Watch out for the Marie Blanque they all told me as I left on my final trip – that one's a killer! Thanks to these words my heart was already pounding with anticipation as I arrived at the base; this was one climb I couldn't wait to get my teeth into. Leave Escot heading east and the first kilometre is a gentle 2%, and then the next averages 3%, as does the one after that – um, it's no killer yet. The suspense is really building now, nerves start to creep in – I'm no mathematician, but in order to achieve a final average of over 8% then things will have to pick up very soon or I'll be needing crampons by the end. Tracing the course of the river, with five to go, the slope has risen to 7% but this is still relatively mild; you know it has to get nasty very soon – and so it does. At 3.5 kilometres to go, the touchpaper is lit, the waiting is over. We have lift off! This is what I was warned about: first 8%, and then 10%, and then a whole kilometre of 11% – there are no corners, no distractions – its rage is relentless. OUCH it's hard, all the way to the only hairpin; drag yourself to its apex and then swing round to line up for the summit – just 500m to go but still punishingly steep to the top of a savage road with such a nice name.

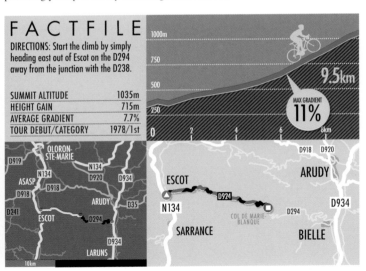

FACTFILE

DIRECTIONS: Start the climb by simply heading east out of Escot on the D294 away from the junction with the D238.

SUMMIT ALTITUDE	1035m
HEIGHT GAIN	715m
AVERAGE GRADIENT	7.7%
TOUR DEBUT/CATEGORY	1978/1st

9.5km

MAX GRADIENT
11%

4 Col d'Aubisque

This is one of the big ones: a legend of the Tour and a climb that's been included in almost every edition in the modern era. I chose the western side as it offers the longest stretch of continuous climbing (unlike the eastern side, which is up and down, taking in the Col du Soulor on its way). Leaving Laruns, cross the bridge, rise up and round the large bend and then head left at the junction. It's a steady start, great for getting the body acclimatized, so try to relax: let your shoulders drop, rest your hands gently on the bars and channel everything into your legs. Four kilometres in, though, the slope ramps up forcing you to tighten your grip as you push through Eaux-Bonnes. Ride up the right-hand side of its one-way system, and then back down the left before heading out of the town where – BOOM – you're stopped in your tracks by a 13% wall. From here on in it's hard work right to the top. Kilometres of 8, 9 and even 10% gradient await you with little or no relief. Continually twisting and turning, this mighty climb finishes in the shadow of three giant bicycles – yellow, green, and of course polka-dotted – which dwarf everything apart from the colossal mountains that surround you.

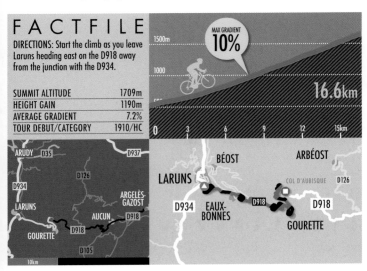

FACTFILE

DIRECTIONS: Start the climb as you leave Laruns heading east on the D918 away from the junction with the D934.

SUMMIT ALTITUDE	1709m
HEIGHT GAIN	1190m
AVERAGE GRADIENT	7.2%
TOUR DEBUT/CATEGORY	1910/HC

MAX GRADIENT
10%

1500m

1000

16.6km

0   3   6   9   12   15km

ARUDY   D35   D937
D934   D126
LARUNS   ARGELÈS-GAZOST
AUCUN   D918
GOURETTE   D918
D105
10km

BÉOST   ARBÉOST
LARUNS   COL D'AUBISQUE   D126
D934   EAUX-BONNES   D918   D918
GOURETTE

5 Col du Soulor

The Col du Soulor is rarely ridden alone, as it forms the first two-thirds of the eastern flank of the mighty Col de l'Aubisque. You could say it has been assimilated into its giant neighbour – robbed of its identity, its pride – to become nothing more than a stepping stone to greater things ahead. Well, I want to restore some of that pride – to remove it from the Aubisque and let it stand on its own two feet. Officially you start the climb in Argelès-Gazost, but riding through the first 12 kilometres of 1 to 2% gradient is like sitting through the adverts before a movie; you just want the action to start, and it finally kicks in when you reach Arrens-Marsous. Bending right through town, the road rears up and it's a shock to the system – only 6% to begin with, but soon touching 8% as you twist left, then right, then left through the pastoral land. With 4 kilometres to go, there's a nasty 20% ramp, but save the heroics because, although short, it delivers you into three solid kilometres of 8.5% climbing. This finale is why the Col du Soulor deserves to stand alone – it is a punishing fight through beautifully rugged terrain to the summit, which lies under the gaze of the rocky peaks ahead.

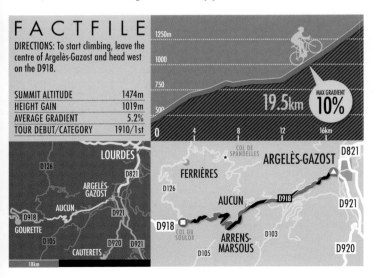

FACTFILE

DIRECTIONS: To start climbing, leave the centre of Argelès-Gazost and head west on the D918.

SUMMIT ALTITUDE	1474m
HEIGHT GAIN	1019m
AVERAGE GRADIENT	5.2%
TOUR DEBUT/CATEGORY	1910/1st

19.5km   MAX GRADIENT 10%

6 Hautacam

First included in 1994, the vicious slopes up to Hautacam are a recent but already infamous part of Tour history. Starting the climb from the roundabout where the D913 leaves the D821 you head east, and then take the second left turn. What follows is a bit complicated but it is signposted – left, then right, then right again and already pretty stiff on a 7% slope. As the incline creeps up to 9% you'll soon find yourself in difficulty, but luckily the steep sections are interspersed at regular intervals with short, shallow stretches to refresh the legs a little. Passing through the village of Artalens there's a wonderful swooping dip: I suggest you enjoy it, as you're about to enter hell. First 9.5%, then 9%, then 10% – the true nature of Hautacam rears its head, and you've 7 kilometres of leg-breaking climbing in front of you. The scenery is truly beautiful and the road does meander wonderfully across the mountainside, but these distractions are still not enough to take away the suffering. Of course, like all climbs, it's worth the effort and the final kilometre backs off to just 6% freeing your legs to finish with a flourish at a giant tarmacked platform affording a view over the whole of the western Pyrenees.

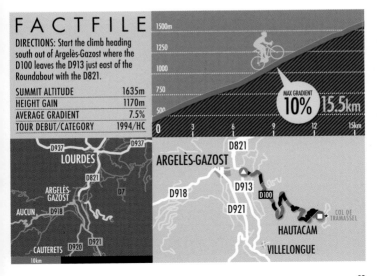

FACTFILE

DIRECTIONS: Start the climb heading south out of Argelès-Gazost where the D100 leaves the D913 just east of the Roundabout with the D821.

SUMMIT ALTITUDE	1635m
HEIGHT GAIN	1170m
AVERAGE GRADIENT	7.5%
TOUR DEBUT/CATEGORY	1994/HC

MAX GRADIENT **10%** 15.5km

LOURDES
D937
D937
D821
ARGELÈS-GAZOST
D7
AUCUN
D918
CAUTERETS
D920
D921
10km

D821
ARGELÈS-GAZOST
D918
D913
D100
D921
HAUTACAM
VILLELONGUE
COL DE TRAMASSEL

7 Luz Ardiden

This is one climb I couldn't wait to ride, as events that took place here during Stage 16 of the 1990 Tour played a key part in forming my love of cycling. On that day Greg Lemond was in imperious form, soaring up the climb with eventually only one man able to hold his pace – the mighty Miguel Indurain. In the final metres, as Lemond's head dropped, Indurain rode away – his graceful yet crushing acceleration and the flourish of his raised arm as he crossed the line are images I will never forget. Needless to say I arrived at the base like a child on Christmas Day and hit the slope hard, as it ramped up steeply out of Luz-Saint-Sauveur. There's no real difficulty until you reach the village of Sazos but from there it's tough the rest of the way. Yes, there are a few flat corners, places to take a short breather, but only a few: this is the Pyrenees remember, there's no such thing as an easy climb. With 4 kilometres to go, I was gutted to lose visibility as I wouldn't see those final bends – in fact the cloud was so thick I was having trouble seeing my handlebars. I just had to push on, left at the junction with 1,500m to go and into the final hairpins where, using my imagination to fill in my surroundings, I did my best to mimic Indurain as I reached the summit.

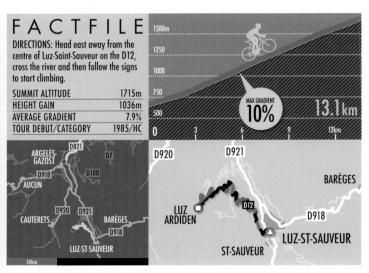

FACTFILE

DIRECTIONS: Head east away from the centre of Luz-Saint-Sauveur on the D12, cross the river and then follow the signs to start climbing.

SUMMIT ALTITUDE	1715m
HEIGHT GAIN	1036m
AVERAGE GRADIENT	7.9%
TOUR DEBUT/CATEGORY	1985/HC

MAX GRADIENT
10%

13.1km

8 Col du Tourmalet

No other climb encapsulates the Tour more than the mighty Tourmalet, which has been incorporated over 80 times since its initial inclusion when the race first entered the high mountains. Popular from both directions, I decided the western side from Luz-Saint-Sauveur was for me and set off fearful of what lay ahead on the highest pass of the Pyrenees. It's not tough to begin with, but once you reach the village of Barèges you pick up the unwelcomingly familiar 9% Pyrenean gradient. Leave the village and OUCH, you hit a 500m sheer wall, and glancing ahead you see the road begin to zigzag upwards. Passing a vast car park, you leave civilization behind and head into the wild, back on yourself, through bend after bend into more 8 and 9% climbing. The slope just keeps hitting you hard – the more dramatic the scenery, the more violent the incline – back and forth you grind up the road as it cuts its way through the savagely primaeval landscape. Delivering the killer blow, the final punishing kilometre – set on a 10% average – takes you to the tiny summit beneath the statue of Octave Lapize, the first rider to conquer this icon of the Tour and who famously dubbed the race organizers 'murderers' for including such a road.

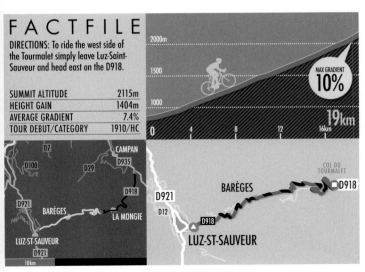

FACTFILE

DIRECTIONS: To ride the west side of the Tourmalet simply leave Luz-Saint-Sauveur and head east on the D918.

SUMMIT ALTITUDE	2115m
HEIGHT GAIN	1404m
AVERAGE GRADIENT	7.4%
TOUR DEBUT/CATEGORY	1910/HC

MAX GRADIENT **10%**

19km

9 Col d'Aspin

It was on the 21st of July 1910 – arguably the most infamous day in Tour history – that the race first headed over the high passes of the Pyrenees and the spectacle we all relish today was born. Travelling from east to west on dreadfully surfaced roads, the first climb on the menu was the Col d'Peyresourde, which was then followed by this climb: the Col d'Aspin. One guidebook describes this as an easy Pyrenean climb, but I'm afraid I'm going to have to correct that. 'Easy' and 'Pyrenean' simply do not, and cannot, inhabit the same space in this or any universe – they form the very definition of 'mutually exclusive'. To its credit, the start is gentle: lined with neat yet overgrown stone walls, the road winds upwards on a 3 to 5% slope. But this easy introduction doesn't last. It's not long before you are toiling away on a 7% slope, and then things turn nasty as 7% rises to 9%. On paper the rest of the climb doesn't seem so bad – it's all under 8% – but in reality it's a brute. You can barely imagine how hard it must have been for the Tour pioneers as they dragged their heavy bikes over gravel roads, picking their way up to the expansive summit, with three giant passes still ahead.

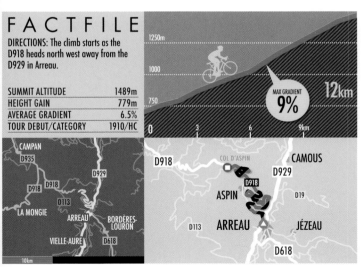

FACTFILE

DIRECTIONS: The climb starts as the D918 heads north west away from the D929 in Arreau.

SUMMIT ALTITUDE	1489m
HEIGHT GAIN	779m
AVERAGE GRADIENT	6.5%
TOUR DEBUT/CATEGORY	1910/HC

MAX GRADIENT 9%

12km

10 Pla d'Adet

On top of the huge bluff, overlooking the vast valley below like a modern-day Machu Picchu, stands the ski station of Pla d'Adet. Approaching the roundabout at its base, you are confronted with the terrifying sight of the road, slashed out of the mountainside, veering skyward. Take a final deep breath and head upwards. Kilometre one is just 6% – so far, so good – but then it ramps up to 12.5%, back to 8, followed by MORE 12.5%. At 5 kilometres in, you reach the village of Saint-Lary-Soulan where, if someone had offered, I'd have swapped my bike for the price of a cold beer – I'd had enough. With morale at rock bottom I was saved by a small plateau, which was just long enough to stop my lungs burning, before it was back on to an 11% slope. If I were a racehorse I'd have been shot, and I was struggling so much it would have come as blessed relief from this infernal torment. But relief, fortunately, does come in the shape of a blissful descent, which brings to an end seven of the toughest kilometres in this book. Here the road doubles back for the final ascent. At ONLY 9% it's a walk in the park, but you'll still just want it to end, and so it does – not in a city of gold, just in a boarded up, out-of-season ski resort.

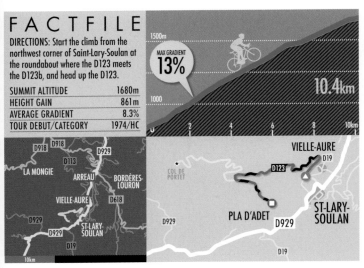

FACTFILE

DIRECTIONS: Start the climb from the northwest corner of Saint-Lary-Soulan at the roundabout where the D123 meets the D123b, and head up the D123.

SUMMIT ALTITUDE	1680m
HEIGHT GAIN	861m
AVERAGE GRADIENT	8.3%
TOUR DEBUT/CATEGORY	1974/HC

MAX GRADIENT **13%**

10.4km

1500m

1000

2 4 6 8 10km

D918 D918 D929
D113
LA MONGIE ARREAU D929
BORDÈRES-LOURON
VIELLE-AURE D618
D929
D929 ST-LARY-SOULAN
D19
10km

VIELLE-AURE
D19
COL DE PORTET
D123
PLA D'ADET
D929 D929
ST-LARY-SOULAN
D19

11 Col d'Azet

As you leave the small village of Génos, which lies at the base of the eastern side of the Col d'Azet, see if you can find somewhere safe to leave your brain – you'll not want it bothering you as you battle up this evil ascent. Signposted 'Val Louron', the start is freakishly difficult: it says 8% but it's harder, and any Tour de France peloton hitting this slope would be shattered like a pane of glass dropped from a ten-storey building. As the sprinters are dropped like hot stones, the elite climbers catapult upwards into the first of fourteen wonderful hairpins. Ascending on a hellish 10% slope, you're already way above Génos and climbing fast – no, make that climbing very, very slowly. With 3 kilometres to go, the frequency of the bends subsides, and you begin a more direct route out of the valley through the beautiful scenery before, at 2 kilometres to go, the road splits. Straight on takes you to Val Louron, which hosted a stage finish in 1991, but you want to head right to continue to the summit. The bracken-lined road, crumbling at the edges, is steep once more through the final bend beneath the ring of jagged peaks lining the horizon. What a tough, tough little climb.

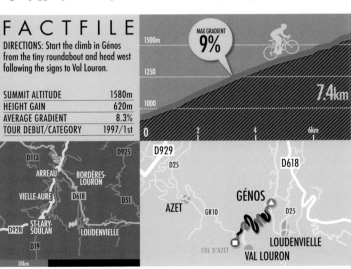

FACTFILE

DIRECTIONS: Start the climb in Génos from the tiny roundabout and head west following the signs to Val Louron.

MAX GRADIENT
9%

1500m

1250

1000

0   2   4   6km

7.4km

SUMMIT ALTITUDE	1580m
HEIGHT GAIN	620m
AVERAGE GRADIENT	8.3%
TOUR DEBUT/CATEGORY	1997/1st

D113 D925
ARREAU BORDÈRES-LOURON
VIELLE-AURE D618 D51
D928 ST-LARY-SOULAN LOUDENVIELLE
D19
10km

D929
D25
D618
AZET GÉNOS
GR10 D25
COL D'AZET LOUDENVIELLE
VAL LOURON

12 Col de Peyresourde

I've already mentioned that day in 1910 when the race first entered the Pyrenees, so just imagine you're riding the Tour that year: chances are you've never even seen a mountain pass, but now you're going to ride over not one, but five, starting with this, the Col d'Peyresourde. Thankfully it's neither the toughest nor the highest climb in the Pyrenees, but that would have been of little comfort to those about to ride it for the very first time – set to take that giant leap into the unknown. Heading west out of Bagnères-de-Luchon, you've a solid kilometre of 8% gradient to start with, leading to a prolonged gentle stretch where your legs can recover. There's a small tangle of bends at roughly one-third distance, but what characterizes the lower slopes are the long, demanding steep straights followed by small levels. First up to Saint-Aventin, and then Cathervielle, and thirdly Portet-de-Luchon – the road resembles a giant flight of stairs heading towards the grassy peaks on the ridge ahead. With 5 kilometres to go, there's a junction where you split off to the right, and before long the fantastic finale comes into view. Up ahead lies a beautifully constructed set of switchbacks perfectly positioned on the smooth slope, ominous in appearance but in reality never too hard to ride.

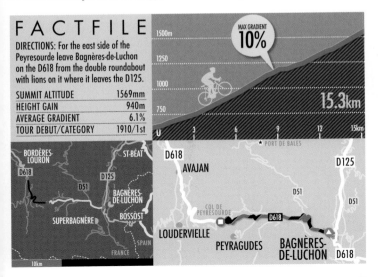

FACTFILE

DIRECTIONS: For the east side of the Peyresourde leave Bagnères-de-Luchon on the D618 from the double roundabout with lions on it where it leaves the D125.

SUMMIT ALTITUDE	1569mm
HEIGHT GAIN	940m
AVERAGE GRADIENT	6.1%
TOUR DEBUT/CATEGORY	1910/1st

MAX GRADIENT
10%

15.3km

★ PORT DE BALES

BORDÈRES-LOURON
ST-BÉAT
D618
D51
D125
BAGNÈRES-DE-LUCHON
SUPERBAGNÈRE
BOSSÒST
SPAIN
FRANCE
10km

D618
AVAJAN
D125
D51
D51
COL DE PEYRESOURDE
D618
LOUDERVIELLE
PEYRAGUDES
BAGNÈRES-DE-LUCHON
D618

13 Port de Balès

I wish I'd had time to ride both sides of this incredible climb. All the way down the southern face I kept saying, 'oh, this is good', 'this side is much better', 'this is brilliant', but the Tour has only ever climbed the northern side, so that's what I chose for the book. Leaving the tiny town of Mauléon-Barousse, there's a short, sharp ramp, and then the slope fades to rise ever so gently following the stream, up and down for a good 8 kilometres before the serious climbing starts. At this point you cross a small bridge and face a junction with no signs; momentarily you are lost in the silence of the forest but logic says left, and logic is correct. Hidden among the dark trees and jagged rocks, the narrow, rugged slope kicks up viciously with kilometres of 10 and 11% gradient but thankfully each one leads to some gentle climbing. Steep, shallow, steep, shallow – the pattern repeats through the isolated forest until, with 2.5 kilometres to ride, you reach a gap in the rock. Instantly the scenery changes, the sky opens, and the claustrophobia of the trees is replaced by the freedom of luscious, green rolling hills, which create a stunning backdrop for the finale, through the last few bends to the exposed summit.

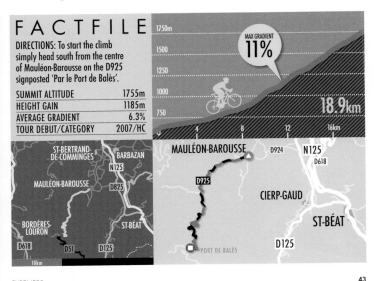

FACTFILE

DIRECTIONS: To start the climb simply head south from the centre of Mauléon-Barousse on the D925 signposted 'Par le Port de Balès'.

SUMMIT ALTITUDE	1755m
HEIGHT GAIN	1185m
AVERAGE GRADIENT	6.3%
TOUR DEBUT/CATEGORY	2007/HC

MAX GRADIENT **11%**

18.9km

MAULÉON-BAROUSSE

PORT DE BALÈS

14 Superbagnères

I wanted to leave this page blank, as I'd prefer to erase all memory of my time on Superbagnères – it broke me, ruined me – more of which I mention in the introduction (see page 11). Hard out of Bagnères-de-Luchon there are some cruel ramps in the first 6 kilometres but these are contained within mostly gentle climbing. Reaching a junction, take the right-hand fork across a bridge and things begin to turn nasty. Up to 8%, then 9%, on and on out of the valley, predominantly straight, but always tough, wearing you down, weakening you before coming in for the kill. The next significant change in direction comes with 8 kilometres to go – sweep round to the right, and up above on a clear day you'll catch sight of the mountain's balding slopes. Hovering around the 8% mark, but touching 10% in places, it's a solid slog as overhead the omnipresent griffon vultures circle, tracking your slowing progress. Twisting back and forth, this brutal road snakes its way across the barren slopes, bend after bend, amid the dazzling scenery. Finally, the giant Grand Hotel appears over a brow, and you've almost made it to the end of this crushing, soul-destroying monster of a climb.

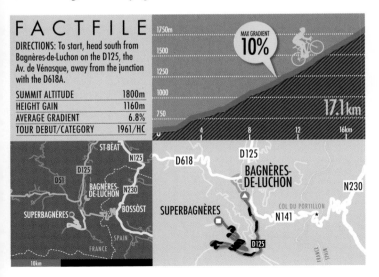

FACTFILE

DIRECTIONS: To start, head south from Bagnères-de-Luchon on the D125, the Av. de Vénasque, away from the junction with the D618A.

SUMMIT ALTITUDE	1800m
HEIGHT GAIN	1160m
AVERAGE GRADIENT	6.8%
TOUR DEBUT/CATEGORY	1961/HC

MAX GRADIENT **10%**

17.1km

1750m
1500m
1250m
1000m
750m

0   4   8   12   16km

ST-BÉAT
N125
D125
D51
BAGNÈRES-DE-LUCHON   N230
SUPERBAGNÈRES   BOSSÒST
SPAIN
FRANCE
10km

D618   D125
BAGNÈRES-DE-LUCHON   N230
SUPERBAGNÈRES   COL DU PORTILLON
N141   ★
D125   FRANCE SPAIN

15 Col du Portillon

Europe's national borders are rarely marked with fanfare. If you're lucky, there may be a sign welcoming you to a new and exotic nation, but more than likely the transition between states will be marked with nothing at all. The Col de Portillon, sneaking out the back of Bagnères-de-Luchon, rises 10 kilometres to one such junction, which is indicated by little more than a rusty old barrier. The first 3 kilometres are easy going, with a protracted opening straight that builds anticipation for what lies ahead. Through a right-hand hairpin and you've the first shocking increase in gradient. It might be just a short climb, but remember where you are: this is the Pyrenees, it is never easy. Fight the slope, which is at times as steep as 14%, through five twisting bends before it straightens up and then eases off again. There are no grand vistas on this climb, neither in front nor behind you, and nothing to divert your attention from the joy of climbing. Push through the steep sections, and then relax on the shallower slopes to leave something in the bank for the punishing finale through two hairpins before lining up for a kilometre of 11 and 9% climbing to the border and down into Spain.

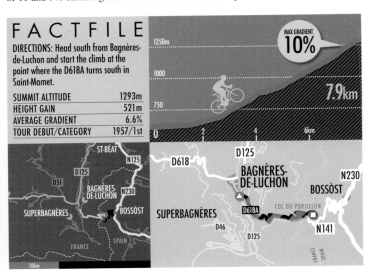

FACTFILE

DIRECTIONS: Head south from Bagnères-de-Luchon and start the climb at the point where the D618A turns south in Saint-Mamet.

SUMMIT ALTITUDE	1293m
HEIGHT GAIN	521m
AVERAGE GRADIENT	6.6%
TOUR DEBUT/CATEGORY	1957/1st

MAX GRADIENT
10%

7.9km

1250m
1000
750

0   2   4   6km

ST-BÉAT
N125
D125
D51
BAGNÈRES-DE-LUCHON
N230
SUPERBAGNÈRES
BOSSÒST
FRANCE   SPAIN
10km

D618
D125
BAGNÈRES-DE-LUCHON
COL DU PORTILLON
N230
BOSSÒST
SUPERBAGNÈRES
D618A
D46
D125
N141
FRANCE SPAIN

16 Col de Menté

Set at the sides of the roads along the majority of climbs in this book are markers that count the kilometres up or down and display other vital statistics such as average gradient and height. On a good day they make fantastic carrots to aim for, but on a bad day the last thing you need to know is, for example, that there are 15 kilometres to go and the next one will average 12%! In this particular region of the Pyrenees, the only information you're offered is one large sign at the base, and then another one 3 kilometres from the top; on the Col de Menté this is a good thing because if you knew how steep each subsequent kilometre was going to be you'd probably turn round and find an easier route over the ridge. Kicking off from Saint-Béat it's straight into 1,500m of 10% gradient, and then it eases a little before you hit two even harder kilometres of 11% climbing. Six kilometres in, through the 'easy' 9% middle section followed by yet more 10% incline, the road begins to twist and turn. I'm not sure what the collective noun for hairpins is. A 'tangle'? A 'wiggle'? Either way, these bends are brilliant, and on a 'mild' 9% slope they form a fantastic finish to this punishing little climb.

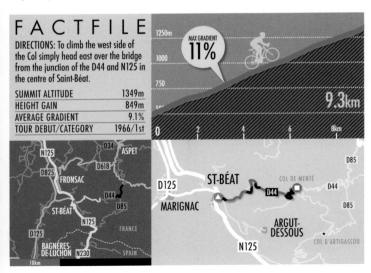

FACTFILE

DIRECTIONS: To climb the west side of the Col simply head east over the bridge from the junction of the D44 and N125 in the centre of Saint-Béat.

SUMMIT ALTITUDE	1349m
HEIGHT GAIN	849m
AVERAGE GRADIENT	9.1%
TOUR DEBUT/CATEGORY	1966/1st

MAX GRADIENT
11%

9.3km

17 Col des Ares

You're in the foothills of the Pyrenees here – the very northern edge of the Massif – and this climb reflects the topography with its uncharacteristically gentle 4% average gradient. Compared with the savage 9% average of the Col de Menté a few kilometres south, it forms a much easier route over this particular ridge. Starting in the east, the climb begins as you cross the river Job heading towards the turn to the village of Cazaunous. It's such a relief to be riding this moderate, uniform incline instead of being stuck in the purgatory of a relentless 9% wall; in fact, it's hard not to get carried away, to get your head down and really give it some stick. Snaking westwards there's only one hairpin, at roughly half distance, where you may need to click down a gear to preserve your cadence before the even consistency of the slope returns. With 500m to go, you pass a sign for a picnic spot where you'll notice it gets somewhat tougher – just enough to make your heart beat that little bit faster. Sprinting for the summit you may even dare to venture on to the big ring but one thing's for sure – you'll be able to give your largest sprockets a rest, and so you should as they're in danger of wearing out in the Pyrenees.

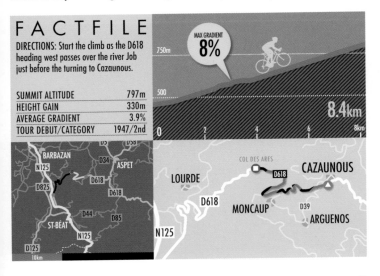

FACTFILE

DIRECTIONS: Start the climb as the D618 heading west passes over the river Job just before the turning to Cazaunous.

MAX GRADIENT **8%**

SUMMIT ALTITUDE	797m
HEIGHT GAIN	330m
AVERAGE GRADIENT	3.9%
TOUR DEBUT/CATEGORY	1947/2nd

8.4km

18 Col de Portet d'Aspet

It is a wonder, when you consider the obvious dangers, that in over 100 years only three riders have died while competing in the Tour de France: Francisco Cepeda in 1935, Tom Simpson in 1967 and Fabio Casartelli as he descended this climb in 1995. I chose to ride the side the Tour went down that tragic year by leaving Aspet on the D5 and climbing gently to the junction with the D618. Winding through the woods and dropping down a couple of times, you reach a small bridge where the road splits and you head left past a sign informing you that the next 4.4 kilometres will average an infernal 9.7%. Clicking down through the gears, the first bend rears up to 20% at its apex and there, as you exit, the striking memorial to Casartelli comes into view; its gleaming white marble set amid the dark forest is such a poignant reminder of the tragedy that you cannot help, especially in your current state of exertion, to be moved. Crawling slowly past, you'll have time to reflect as the punishing gradient continues its remorseless journey upwards. Meandering through the forest, the slope eases only as the trees clear for the milder, but still dragging, final few hundred metres to the summit.

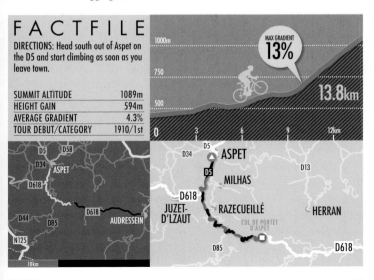

FACTFILE

DIRECTIONS: Head south out of Aspet on the D5 and start climbing as soon as you leave town.

SUMMIT ALTITUDE	1089m
HEIGHT GAIN	594m
AVERAGE GRADIENT	4.3%
TOUR DEBUT/CATEGORY	1910/1st

MAX GRADIENT
13%

13.8km

19 Col de la Core

Enveloped in forest for almost its entire length, the Col de la Core starts in the small town of Les Bordes-sur-Lez on the D17 heading east away from the D4. The overall average gradient is only 5% so you know at the outset that it's no killer but that doesn't mean it fails to pack a punch. Leaving Les Bordes, the slope begins on a stiff 7% for a couple of kilometres before it falls back to just 3% as it ambles in and out of a jumble of small villages. I've only mentioned road surfaces on a couple of other occasions in this book but I must draw attention to this one as well because it is the most abrasive I faced on all the 100 Climbs. On the day I rode, I was lucky enough to have a favorable wind, but any and all assistance I received was directly sucked away as my tyres dragged over the awful, coarse topping. Five kilometres in, the easy climbing is over and things get harder: first 7% then ramping up to 8 for the assault on the summit where the predominantly straight road begins to bend. Through the final kilometres to the grassy peak, the trees fade and you can cast your eyes down over the route you've successfully conquered as it snakes up out of the valley.

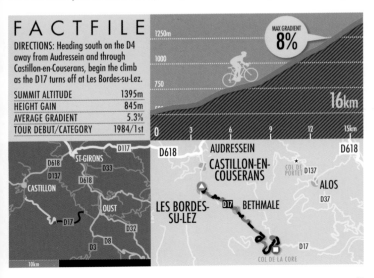

FACTFILE

DIRECTIONS: Heading south on the D4 away from Audressein and through Castillon-en-Couserans, begin the climb as the D17 turns off at Les Bordes-su-Lez.

SUMMIT ALTITUDE	1395m
HEIGHT GAIN	845m
AVERAGE GRADIENT	5.3%
TOUR DEBUT/CATEGORY	1984/1st

MAX GRADIENT **8%**

16km

20 Guzet-Neige

Before Britain began to dominate the world of cycling in the early 21st century, first in the velodromes and then on the road, its victories in the world's greatest races were few and far between. One elusive triumph did come here, though, at Guzet-Neige when, in 1984, Scotland's Robert Millar won the stage and also claimed the King of the Mountains polka-dot jersey to boot. There are two ways to begin: either from Aulus-les-Bains in the east via the Col de Latrape, or – the way I rode – by leaving Sérac d'Ustou in the west. Directly ahead, right from the start, you see the Guzet-Neige ski resort nestled in the trees on top of the mountain, so start weaving up to where the two beginnings meet. Separating from the D8, you dip down to the right to embark on the final tough kilometres. Set on a slope that hovers around a punishing 8% all the way, it seems an unlikely spot for skiing and it's not until you close in on Guzet that you see the first evidence of any winter pastime: a line of chairlifts straddling the ridge. With 1,500m to ride, you begin your way up through the resort; just keep riding, through a jumble of bends until you can go no further, to a dead end in yet another seasonally abandoned ski resort.

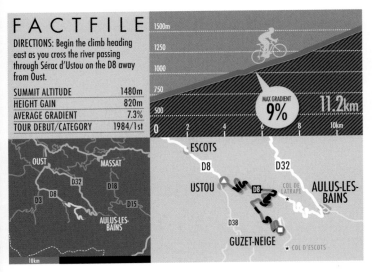

FACTFILE

DIRECTIONS: Begin the climb heading east as you cross the river passing through Sérac d'Ustou on the D8 away from Oust.

SUMMIT ALTITUDE	1480m
HEIGHT GAIN	820m
AVERAGE GRADIENT	7.3%
TOUR DEBUT/CATEGORY	1984/1st

MAX GRADIENT **9%**   **11.2km**

1500m
1250
1000
750
500

0   2   4   6   8   10km

OUST   MASSAT
D32   D18
D8
D3   D15
AULUS-LES-BAINS
10km

ESCOTS
D8   D32
USTOU   D8   COL DE LATRAPE   AULUS-LES-BAINS
D38
GUZET-NEIGE   ★ COL D'ESCOTS

21 Col de Latrape

Huddled in the bottom of the valley at the base of two climbs – the Col d'Agnes and the Col de Latrape – lies the small spa town of Aulus-les-Bains. Built around thermal springs, this town is a perfect place to base yourself for a day's climbing. Head east to make the Col de Latrape the first climb of the day – in places very sharp, shock, which also offers the bonus of a ride up to Guzet-Neige if you keep on travelling over the summit. When you hit the base after arriving from the flat valley floor, your speed will be checked, like a skydiver opening a parachute during free fall, as you begin the 8% slope out of town. Up hard, and then even harder into the second kilometre, which peaks at a very solid 10% before easing slightly through a kilometre of 6 and 7% gradient. While riding, the differences in the slope are hard to notice; it all feels pretty hard from base to summit through four hairpins, but the variations are there if you concentrate. Take a moment to get your breath back in the middle, and rest your legs before the finale where the slope again ramps up to 10%, eventually settling down to 8% to finish a kilometre shy of the left-hand turn to Guzet-Neige, and then more climbing.

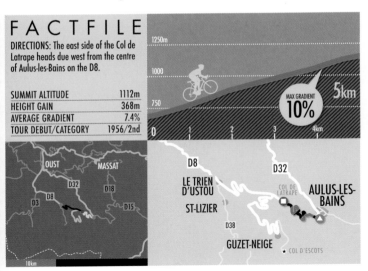

FACTFILE

DIRECTIONS: The east side of the Col de Latrape heads due west from the centre of Aulus-les-Bains on the D8.

SUMMIT ALTITUDE	1112m
HEIGHT GAIN	368m
AVERAGE GRADIENT	7.4%
TOUR DEBUT/CATEGORY	1956/2nd

MAX GRADIENT
10%

5km

1250m
1000
750
0   1   2   3   4km

OUST   MASSAT
D32   D18
D8
D3   D15
10km

D8
LE TRIEN
D'USTOU
ST-LIZIER

D32
COL DE
LATRAPE

AULUS-LES-
BAINS

D38
GUZET-NEIGE   ★ COL D'ESCOTS

22 Col d'Agnes

I loved this climb – loved it. Maybe I had good legs, maybe after five days in the Pyrenees I'd acclimatized to the ridiculous 9 and 10% gradients – either way, the Col d'Agnes was a pleasure to ride. Leaving Aulus-les-Bains, heading south-east, you've 500m to get your affairs in order – to take a drink, tighten your shoe buckles – before the road bends sharp right into 3 bends of over 10% climbing. Rising in a straight line following the course of the river, it's a gruelling start that eases only a fraction to 9% over the following 4 kilometres. Not until the climb approaches the first of seven majestic hairpins does the punishing slope release its grip and drop down to a manageable 7%, allowing you a brief moment to take stock. First bending left, the tight bends are very welcome as they take the sting out of the incline, and then with 2 kilometres to go, the slope backs off even more. You'll feel reborn and able to pick up some speed as you leave the forest to cast your eyes over the grandeur of the valley you've escaped. It's not all plain sailing, though: there is a little more 10% to come in the finale, but you'll breeze through this to finish on the level between rocky outcrops.

FACTFILE

DIRECTIONS: To climb, simply head south out of the centre of Aulus-les-Bains on the D81.

SUMMIT ALTITUDE	1570m
HEIGHT GAIN	826m
AVERAGE GRADIENT	8.1%
TOUR DEBUT/CATEGORY	1988/1st

MAX GRADIENT
10%

10.2km

23 Port de Lers

Not the hardest, not the longest, nor the steepest, but for a long stretch this felt like the most pleasant road I'd ridden anywhere especially on a warm, late summer's day. Leave the junction of the D8 and D18 in Vicdessos and twist your way out of town, heading north-west to begin a not-quite-so-charming and increasingly hard dead-straight prelude to the beauty ahead. Grinding upwards, you'll soon be free of this punishing start, but there's a wicked little 15% ramp to master before the road's character changes instantly. In a flash – wide, open, and steep are replaced by narrow, covered, and shallow, and here's where the charm of this climb reveals itself. Picking your way upwards across the dappled sunlight that illuminates the gnarled surface, instead of being accompanied by the usual sound of laboured breathing, the air is filled with feverish birdsong and flowing waterfalls: you've arrived slap bang in the middle of a true woodland paradise. Hovering around the 6% mark, the gradient plays its part in creating heaven, but with 2.5 kilometres to go, everything changes once more as the climb does what all Pyrenean roads should do by ramping up to 9% and switching back and forth on its push to peak on the open summit.

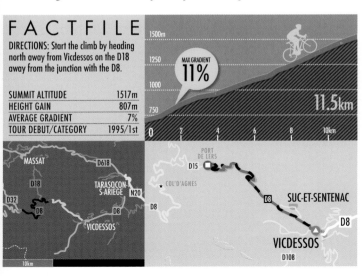

FACTFILE

DIRECTIONS: Start the climb by heading north away from Vicdessos on the D18 away from the junction with the D8.

SUMMIT ALTITUDE	1517m
HEIGHT GAIN	807m
AVERAGE GRADIENT	7%
TOUR DEBUT/CATEGORY	1995/1st

MAX GRADIENT **11%**

1500m
1250
1000
750

11.5km

0   2   4   6   8   10km

MASSAT   D618   D18   TARASCON-S-ARIEGE   N20   D32   D8   VICDESSOS   10km

PORT DE LERS   D15   COL D'AGNES   D8   SUC-ET-SENTENAC   D8   VICDESSOS   D8   D108

24 Mur de Péguère

Mur is French for wall, which should tell you pretty much all you need to know about this vicious little road, but besides being terribly steep, why, when it's only 3.6 kilometres long, did I include it in this book? Well, of course, the climb was used in the Tour – just the once in 2012 – when it earned its notoriety after local farmers opposed to the reintroduction of bears to the mountains covered it with carpet tacks. By bringing more than one of the favourites to a grinding halt, the debate captured the public's attention. And it is a topic that cannot be avoided as virtually every road in the region is daubed with the giant slogan 'OURS NON' or 'NO BEARS'. Leaving the D618 at the peak of the Col des Caugnous, the sign in front of you displays the cold hard facts of what lies ahead: 3.6 kilometres at an average gradient of 11.8% and a maximum of 18%! The first kilometre is the hardest – averaging over 14% – but the views to the right are just brilliant; next you reach the left-hand bend where the slope calms down to only 11%. Ignore your screaming legs and fight the incline for two infernal kilometres to reach the right-hand bend and the final gruelling push to the summit to finish exhausted but hopefully with both tyres intact.

FACTFILE

DIRECTIONS: Start the tiny climb as you head north away from the D618 and ride the short distance up to the D17.

SUMMIT ALTITUDE	1375m
HEIGHT GAIN	418m
AVERAGE GRADIENT	12%
TOUR DEBUT/CATEGORY	2012/1st

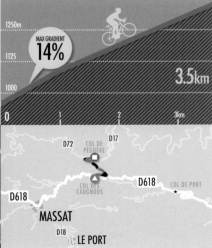

MAX GRADIENT **14%**

3.5km

25 Col de Port

How bland the world would be if everything were the same – if no one broke the mould, dared to be different, or, in the case of Pyrenean climbs, stuck remorselessly to that infernal 9% incline. Well, thank goodness for the Col de Port, a climb that never, not even once, rises above 7% and in doing so becomes something I never thought I'd find: a gentle Pyrenean climb. Of course it's no breeze and I attach the moniker 'gentle' in the context of its contemporaries; it is simply refreshing to use a few different gears rather than having the chain glued to the 27 all day. Start the climb by dropping down the short descent from Massat, and then, carrying that speed, hit the slope and settle into the metronomic rhythm that will haul you all the way to the top. There are plenty of bends to occupy you on the course upwards but it's easy to daydream now that the mind is free from fighting the constant urge to throw in the towel – to stop the pain. Across the wooded slopes, past the typical dark slate roofs you reach the summit, and, without having to collapse over the bars in an exhausted mess, you are able to stand upright and take in the stunning view out over the eastern Pyrenees.

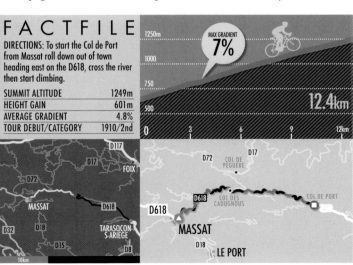

FACTFILE

DIRECTIONS: To start the Col de Port from Massat roll down out of town heading east on the D618, cross the river then start climbing.

SUMMIT ALTITUDE	1249m
HEIGHT GAIN	601m
AVERAGE GRADIENT	4.8%
TOUR DEBUT/CATEGORY	1910/2nd

MAX GRADIENT **7%**

1250m
1000
750
500
0

12.4km

0   3   6   9   12km

26 Plateau du Beille

A firm favourite in recent Tours, the climb up to the Plateau de Beille is as solid as they come, set on an almost constant 8 to 9% gradient. Leaving the centre of Les Cabannes, you bear right and – GULP – it's time to fasten the seat belts as the bold, wide road heads skyward out of town. There are distinct clusters of hairpins to tackle along the route, which never diverts from its course south, and with 9 kilometres in the bag you come face to face with the first stretch of 10% incline. This single-percent increase is enough to tip you into the danger zone so just do your best to get through and return to the 9% norm. Every now and again there are patches where the road eases and your legs are released to spin free – float for a few seconds before the slope bites back. Like a cold drink to a dehydrated man lost in the desert, these sections refresh and restore the body, readying it for more climbing. Up ahead, the large sign welcomes you to the plateau but it's not the top – roll across the large clearing and start climbing again. The finale drags on and on, and even though the gradient eases it's a struggle to finally reach the giant plateau – a lost world in the shadow of mountain peaks, hidden from the valley below.

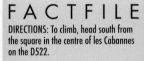

FACTFILE

DIRECTIONS: To climb, head south from the square in the centre of les Cabannes on the D522.

SUMMIT ALTITUDE	1780m
HEIGHT GAIN	1255m
AVERAGE GRADIENT	7.9%
TOUR DEBUT/CATEGORY	1998/HC

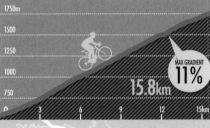

MAX GRADIENT **11%**

15.8km

27 Ax 3 Domaines

You say Plateau de Bonascre; I say Ax 3 Domaines. This climb is known by both titles, the first refers to the plateau at the summit, and the second to the resort you'll find there. Leaving the picturesque banks of the river Oriège in Ax-les-Thermes, head up to the first of six consecutive hairpins lined with houses, before crossing a freshly constructed bridge, and you're free of town. Consistently hard – from 9, to 10, to 11% – the first 2 kilometres, through the wonderfully tight bends, will force you to dig into your reserves to keep pedalling smoothly in order to reach a nice stretch of 6% slope. Free of the corners, the road lines out to a right-hand bend, and then it's straight again up to a second set of six switchbacks – all the way on an evil 10% incline. The road covered with the painted names of riders from recent Tours, you try to make out the fading writing and decipher the messages as you crawl slowly upwards. Another shallow stretch awaits you – longer than the first one – but your new momentum will vanish as you hit the final kilometre into the heart of the resort. Round a tight right-hand bend, then a left – imagine the crowds, the colour and the noise as you roll over the brow to finish at a dead end.

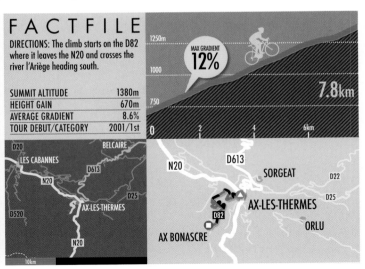

FACTFILE

DIRECTIONS: The climb starts on the D82 where it leaves the N20 and crosses the river l'Ariège heading south.

SUMMIT ALTITUDE	1380m
HEIGHT GAIN	670m
AVERAGE GRADIENT	8.6%
TOUR DEBUT/CATEGORY	2001/1st

MAX GRADIENT **12%**

7.8km

1250m
1000
750
0   2   4   6km

D20   BELCAIRE
LES CABANNES
D613
N20
D25
AX-LES-THERMES
D520
N20
10km

N20   D613
SORGEAT   D22
D25
AX-LES-THERMES
D82
ORLU
AX BONASCRE

28 Port de Pailhères

WOW. This is the road I dream of at night, this is the road I'll be riding for all eternity when my time comes to leave this world – this is hill climbing, hairpin, heaven. It's a road-building masterpiece without equal; if you had purpose-built a mountain to purpose-build a road up it and could choose any permutation of gradient and twists and turns, this is exactly what you would come up with. The fun begins right away as you leave Mijanès through a couple of 20% switchbacks, and once free of town the road rises arrow-straight for a few kilometres, set on a slope just shy of 10%, before dropping back to 8%. Three groups of bends break your journey westwards, and then, with the majority of the climb now under your belt, you arrive in cycling paradise. Up ahead you'll catch sight of the white bollards lining the road that signal the beginning of an amazing, chaotic tangle of climbing joy – left, right, stacked on top of each other, all the way set on a 9 to 10% slope. Further up, and now exposed to the elements, the angle of incline decreases, and those bends – they just keep on coming, almost all the way to the summit, which, as if things couldn't get any better, takes you over the magic 2,000m mark. AWESOME.

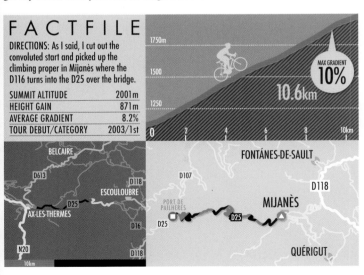

FACTFILE

DIRECTIONS: As I said, I cut out the convoluted start and picked up the climbing proper in Mijanès where the D116 turns into the D25 over the bridge.

SUMMIT ALTITUDE	2001m
HEIGHT GAIN	871m
AVERAGE GRADIENT	8.2%
TOUR DEBUT/CATEGORY	2003/1st

MAX GRADIENT
10%

10.6km

BELCAIRE
D613
ESCOULOUBRE
D118
D25
AX-LES-THERMES
D16
N20
D118

FONTANÉS-DE-SAULT
D107
D118
PORT DE PAILHÈRES
MIJANÈS
D25
D25
QUÉRIGUT

29 Col d'Ordino

Andorra's an odd place. On first approach, heading south from Ax-les-Thermes and once you've negotiated the convoluted route to the border, the buildings that greet you are so utterly grotesque you're half tempted to turn round and head back. Keeping your blinkers on and ignoring the carbuncle of Pas de la Casa with its myriad service stations flogging cheap fuel, just keep going and soon you'll be through to explore the pristine interior. The Col d'Ordino shares its base with the climb on page 76, which rises up to the Arcalís ski station heading south from Ordino, whereas the Arcalís climb heads north. Rising on a 6 to 7% gradient, this climb is typical of a country that appears to be an oasis of moderate gradient set in a mountain range of 9% inclines: a retreat for exhausted legs that have been pummelled to submission on the cruel Pyrenean slopes. Winding through nine wonderful bends, base to summit is spot on 10 kilometres through forest that breaks here and there to expose the stunning scenery surrounding you. You'll never be troubled by the climb, and the road even levels towards the end to allow you a run up at the summit, which lies just round the corner from where you'd hoped it to be.

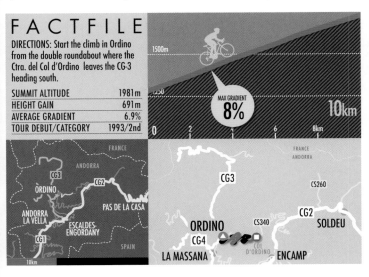

FACTFILE

DIRECTIONS: Start the climb in Ordino from the double roundabout where the Ctra. del Col d'Ordino leaves the CG-3 heading south.

SUMMIT ALTITUDE	1981m
HEIGHT GAIN	691m
AVERAGE GRADIENT	6.9%
TOUR DEBUT/CATEGORY	1993/2nd

MAX GRADIENT
8%

1500m

1250

0   2   6   8km

10km

FRANCE
ANDORRA
CG3
CG2
ÒRDINO
PAS DE LA CASA
ANDORRA
LA VELLA
ESCALDES-
ENGORDANY
CG1
SPAIN
10km

FRANCE
ANDORRA
CG3
CS260
CS340
CG2
ORDINO
CG4
COL
D'ORDINO
SOLDEU
LA MASSANA
ENCAMP

30 Andorre-Arcalís

Arcalís will always hold a special place in my heart, as it was the last climb I rode during an amazing ten-day trip through the Pyrenees while researching this book, with my dad as co-driver. Heading north from Ordino, the road rolls up and down on a shallow slope past the identically immaculate villages, with only the sharp ramp out of La Cortinada to trouble your legs. It's in El Serrat that the proper climbing starts, as you twist through the village round five hairpins on a slope that approaches a whopping 20% in places. For the next 4 kilometres, you have to put a proper shift in, even though the average never climbs above 9%, and then with 5 kilometres to go, passing through a dark tunnel, you enter the world of Arcalís. Unlike any ski resort I'd encountered before, devoid of the usual architectural high-rise disasters, it contains only the bare minimum of paraphernalia to feed and transport skiers up and down the mountain. The final bends to the summit sweep upwards through pristine, breathtakingly beautiful scenery on a similarly luscious 6% incline. I could have ridden them forever, but, alas, the summit and my adventure had to end – as all mountains always, unfortunately, do.

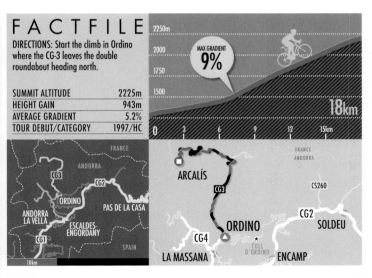

FACTFILE

DIRECTIONS: Start the climb in Ordino where the CG-3 leaves the double roundabout heading north.

SUMMIT ALTITUDE	2225m
HEIGHT GAIN	943m
AVERAGE GRADIENT	5.2%
TOUR DEBUT/CATEGORY	1997/HC

MAX GRADIENT 9%

2250m
2000
1750
1500

18km

0   3   6   9   12   15km

FRANCE
ANDORRA
CG3
CG2
ORDINO
ANDORRA
LA VELLA
PAS DE LA CASA
ESCALDES-ENGORDANY
CG1
SPAIN
10km

FRANCE
ANDORRA
ARCALÍS
CG3
CS260
CG2
SOLDEU
ORDINO
CG4
COLL D'ORDINO
LA MASSANA
ENCAMP

MASSIF
CENTRAL

31 Col de Vendeix

There's more to this region of France than just the Puy de Dôme, but it's impossible to ignore the infamous peak that dominates the horizon, so why, you ask, isn't that climb included in the book? Well, even though it has been ridden many times in the Tour, it is now frustratingly no longer open to cyclists, which is a shame as its spiralled route round the volcanic cone to the summit is just so fantastically unique. But, as I said, there's far more riding to be found in this area – one of the most beautiful parts of the country. This climb, the short but sweet Montée de la Roche Vendeix, rises out of La Bourboule. Starting from the heart of town, the gradient feels testing at first but doesn't get any worse, and settles into a 6% incline as you make your way up and away through the houses that line either side of the road. Ducking in and out of the cover of trees, your route twists a little through a few bends but there's no genuine drama – it is simply a pleasant climb away from a pleasant town in a pleasant part of the world. The summit lies at the junction with the D645, where I would recommend turning left and heading down into Le Mont-Dore to climb up the Col de la Croix Saint-Robert.

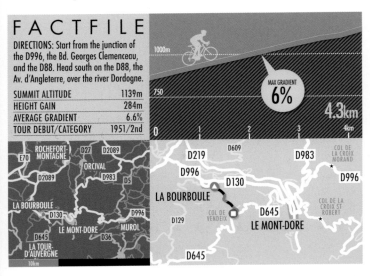

FACTFILE

DIRECTIONS: Start from the junction of the D996, the Bd. Georges Clemenceau, and the D88. Head south on the D88, the Av. d'Angleterre, over the river Dordogne.

SUMMIT ALTITUDE	1139m
HEIGHT GAIN	284m
AVERAGE GRADIENT	6.6%
TOUR DEBUT/CATEGORY	1951/2nd

MAX GRADIENT 6%

4.3km

32 Col de la Croix Saint-Robert

Having no previous knowledge of this area, I was surprised when I arrived in Le Mont-Dore to discover that it was a mini ski town. As the peaks were all at such a modest altitude compared with the Alps, I had assumed they would not amass enough snow to support skiing. However, owing mainly to its central location, this is statistically the coldest region in the whole of France. But I wasn't here to marvel at the local climate: there was a climb to be tackled, so to start I left town up the stiff Avenue Georges Clemenceau, and then took the first left towards two micro hairpins. Passing a large sign that proudly advertises the climb's statistics, including the fact that it is 5.8 kilometres to the summit, it's not long before you're rising above Le Mont-Dore into the toughest part of the road, set on an 8% gradient. This will leave your legs sore as you exit the woodland to ride across an open plateau, surrounded by the wonderful grass-covered volcanic peaks that ring the horizon. Ride through the clearing into some switchbacks, and then you exit for the sedate journey to the summit, which lies in a place of immense calm and beauty, nestled between two perfectly smooth grassy mounds.

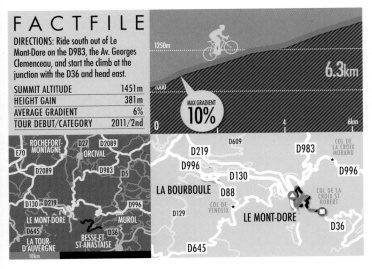

FACTFILE

DIRECTIONS: Ride south out of Le Mont-Dore on the D983, the Av. Georges Clemenceau, and start the climb at the junction with the D36 and head east.

SUMMIT ALTITUDE	1451m
HEIGHT GAIN	381m
AVERAGE GRADIENT	6%
TOUR DEBUT/CATEGORY	2011/2nd

MAX GRADIENT
10%

1250m

1000

0

4

6km

6.3km

ROCHEFORT-MONTAGNE D27 D2089 ORCIVAL D609 D219 COL DE LA CROIX MORAND D983
E70 D2089 D983 D5 D996 D996 D130 D996
D130 D219 LA BOURBOULE D88 COL DE LA CROIX ST ROBERT
LE MONT-DORE D645 D129 COL DE VENDEIX LE MONT-DORE
LA TOUR-D'AUVERGNE BESSE-ET-ST-ANASTAISE MUROL D36 D36
10km D645

33 Col de la Croix Morand

It's hard to pin down the exact start of this climb but the logical spot seems to be Chambon-sur-Lac, and leaving town the road immediately ramps up a challenging 8% slope to test the legs. Next you double back on yourself, round a tight hairpin, and the gradient settles into the 5 to 6% incline that will take you most of the way to the top. Through patchy woodland, and then out across open grassland you meander upwards with little or no difficulty, just efficiently ticking off the kilometres one by one. And then the 1-kilometre-to-go sign comes into view – you can taste the summit now; right on cue the body releases the burst of adrenaline it's been holding in reserve to carry you there, a kick of mental energy to ignite the afterburners for the final push to the top. This particular sign, however, states that the final kilometre will be run on a 3% slope, but quite frankly that's nonsense: it's more like 8%, and this wipes away your newly found speed to bring you crashing back to earth. The last stretch of the climb is beautifully exposed, and if there's any wind it will either blow you up or stop you in your tracks, but either way you'll not escape it as you roll to the summit beneath the smooth grassy peaks.

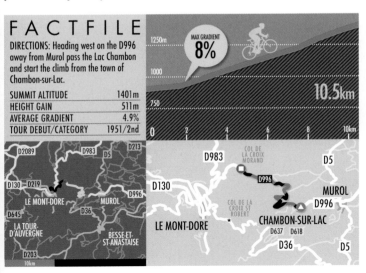

FACTFILE

DIRECTIONS: Heading west on the D996 away from Murol pass the Lac Chambon and start the climb from the town of Chambon-sur-Lac.

SUMMIT ALTITUDE	1401m
HEIGHT GAIN	511m
AVERAGE GRADIENT	4.9%
TOUR DEBUT/CATEGORY	1951/2nd

MAX GRADIENT **8%**

1250m

1000

750

0   2   4   6   8   10km

10.5km

D2089   D983   D5   D213

D130 — D219

LE MONT-DORE   MUROL   D996

D645   D36

LA TOUR-
D'AUVERGNE

D203

10km

BESSE-ET-
ST-ANASTAISE

D983   COL DE LA CROIX MORAND   D5

D130   D996

COL DE LA CROIX ST ROBERT   MUROL   D996

LE MONT-DORE   ★   CHAMBON-SUR-LAC

D637   D618

D36   D5

34 Super-Besse

With its origins way away in the town of Issoire, this climb ambles upwards for many kilometres before the real action starts in Besse-et-Saint-Anastaise. The road picks its way through the quaint town on a slope that touches 20% in places, and then once out of town you reach a junction where you're offered a choice of two routes forward. Logic says head straight on, but this one-way dual carriageway is a bit of a rat run so head left, up and over a small lump, to rejoin the previous route from where you get your first glimpse of what's to come. In front of you stands a formidable stretch of 11% gradient; the engineers did away with the usual switchbacks and just built this road straight up the side of the hill. Ouch, it hurts. There's nothing I hate more than a straight, wide climb and this one's an absolute beast – an evil ramp of pain heading to the sky. When it does end, and the road finally bends, you are broken. Although the curves soften the blow, the gradient doesn't budge until the sign for Super-Besse comes into view. Thankfully, the worst is now over: the incline ebbs away and the road finishes by plateauing just before it reaches the heart of the small resort.

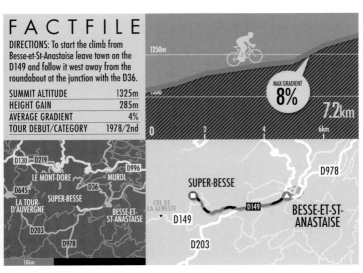

FACTFILE

DIRECTIONS: To start the climb from Besse-et-St-Anastaise leave town on the D149 and follow it west away from the roundabout at the junction with the D36.

SUMMIT ALTITUDE	1325m
HEIGHT GAIN	285m
AVERAGE GRADIENT	4%
TOUR DEBUT/CATEGORY	1978/2nd

MAX GRADIENT **8%**

7.2km

35 Col des Pradeaux

This is everything you could ever want from a climb: beautiful sweeping bends, stunning views and just the most perfect 11.5 kilometres of possibly the smoothest tarmac you'll ever ride. Breaking my own rule of mentioning the condition of the surface – it's like glass, smoother than the proverbial baby's bottom and just heaven under the tyres. Leaving Ambert riding west to east, you rise up then swoop down to start the proper climbing at the bottom of the hollow. Sweeping upwards through the beautiful bends, in and out, back and forth, every revolution of the wheels is a joy – this is why we ride bikes, right here. Hovering around a constant 6% it's not until you've 7 kilometres under your belt that it creeps over 7% but that doesn't last long. There is literally nothing that will taint your experience of this fantastic road. With 2 kilometres to go, the huge radio tower creeps into view, peeking out above the trees and this, unfortunately, signals the arrival of the summit. The Col des Pradeaux is proof, if it were ever needed, that it's not just about the highest, steepest, or the longest climb – sometimes it's just about the sheer pleasure of riding uphill.

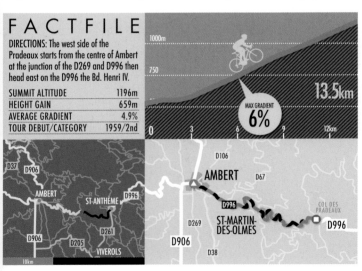

FACTFILE

DIRECTIONS: The west side of the Pradeaux starts from the centre of Ambert at the junction of the D269 and D996 then head east on the D996 the Bd. Henri IV.

SUMMIT ALTITUDE	1196m
HEIGHT GAIN	659m
AVERAGE GRADIENT	4.9%
TOUR DEBUT/CATEGORY	1959/2nd

MAX GRADIENT **6%**

13.5km

36 Col de la Croix de l'Homme Mort

There are two great climbs that link the towns of Montbrison and Ambert: the Col des Pradeaux and this climb, the Col de la Croix de l'Homme Mort – translated, 'dead man's cross'! Heading east to west you begin from the last roundabout at the edge of town to start climbing on a mild gradient, and then following a couple of kilometres you reach a slight dip. It's the perfect climb to start a day's ride as the whole route is set on a 5 to 6% slope with nothing over 7%, so it's never uncomfortable. The omnipresent ridge, lined with conifers, is your target, as you meander through the peaceful farmland, past the villages of Lézigneux and Verrières-en-Forez. Every now and again very subtle changes in the steepness of the slope may force you from the saddle and these tend to become more frequent as you approach the forest ahead. With 3 kilometres left, you ride into the silence of the trees, a shroud of tall, dark conifers that will shelter you from whatever weather you may be experiencing. Slightly steeper up to the final kilometre, and then easing back dramatically, you close in on the summit of this placid climb, which in reality is not nearly as grim as its name implies.

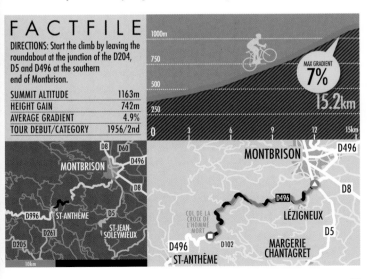

FACTFILE

DIRECTIONS: Start the climb by leaving the roundabout at the junction of the D204, D5 and D496 at the southern end of Montbrison.

SUMMIT ALTITUDE	1163m
HEIGHT GAIN	742m
AVERAGE GRADIENT	4.9%
TOUR DEBUT/CATEGORY	1956/2nd

MAX GRADIENT 7%

15.2km

37 Col de la République

One of the ugliest of roads I've ridden but one of the most significant in Tour history, this was the first-ever climb over 1,000m in the very first tour back in 1903. It's no mountain, but great journeys begin with small steps, and with the riders proving themselves capable, the organizers began to dream of bigger things. Just two years later they included the first real mountain, the Ballon d'Alsace, and then in 1910 the floodgates were well and truly opened with that infamous trek across the Pyrenees. The first 3 kilometres are set on a benign gradient lined with run-down buildings. It's busy, claustrophobic, and not pleasant to ride; however, things do improve. As the slope creeps up to a steady 6%, the route weaves around some more but there are no switchbacks to alter its trajectory south. The incline backs off a little in Planfoy and picks up as it leaves, but then, unfortunately, there are some traffic lights. If you're lucky you will catch them on green to continue along the last of the 6% gradient before it begins to ebb away. The last 6 kilometres never rise above 4% and at times the road appears pan flat. I'm sure it was a big deal back in 1903 but these days it's little more than a lump.

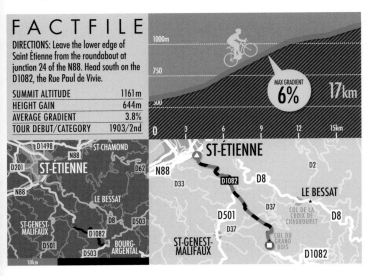

FACTFILE

DIRECTIONS: Leave the lower edge of Saint Étienne from the roundabout at junction 24 of the N88. Head south on the D1082, the Rue Paul de Vivie.

SUMMIT ALTITUDE	1161m
HEIGHT GAIN	644m
AVERAGE GRADIENT	3.8%
TOUR DEBUT/CATEGORY	1903/2nd

MAX GRADIENT **6%**   17km

38 Col de la Croix de Chaubouret

Running parallel to its more famous neighbour, the Col de la République, this climb is far better on all accounts: it's longer, it's steeper, and most importantly it's much quieter. I'd say the only black mark on its report card is that the first 500m are so incredibly hard. Up the vicious ramp, rising away from the bustle of Saint-Étienne, you have to fight like a rocket resisting the pull of gravity to escape the city's grasp. Away from the roundabout, head right at the first junction and then straight on at the next junction, where this baptism of fire comes to an end. It will take a couple of kilometres for the legs to recover from this punishment, but as the rest of the route is significantly easier, recover they do – so you can really enjoy this road. However, it's no walk in the park: rising past the castle ruins in Rochetaillée you hit a tough stretch – a tasty 7% filling in a sandwich of 4% gradient. As you home in on the summit, passing through the one-way streets of Le Bessat, take time to soak in the glorious views of the interlocking hills on your left. This beautiful climb in a beautiful part of the world comes to an end at a large crossroads on an expansive plateau.

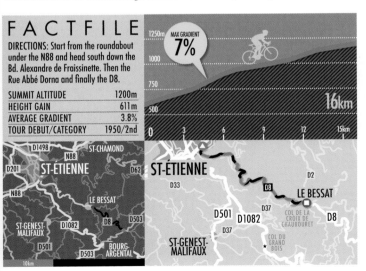

FACTFILE

DIRECTIONS: Start from the roundabout under the N88 and head south down the Bd. Alexandre de Fraissinette. Then the Rue Abbé Dorna and finally the D8.

SUMMIT ALTITUDE	1200m
HEIGHT GAIN	611m
AVERAGE GRADIENT	3.8%
TOUR DEBUT/CATEGORY	1950/2nd

MAX GRADIENT 7%

16km

39 Col de l'Œillon

There are views, there are amazing views, and then there is the view overlooking the vast Rhône valley from the top of the Col de l'Œillon – it will leave you speechless, once you've got to the top that is. The climb starts way down in Chavanay where you begin by heading west up the D7 away from the N86. It's tight through town but not steep, and you soon exit to make your way up the incline to Pélussin. Negotiate its one-way system by keeping an eye on the signs to Le Bessat, and once out of town it's the turn-off on to the D63. Here is where the best part of the climb starts: heading left, away from the main road, it is steep from the junction – you round a few bends, and then over your left shoulder you get your first proper sight of that view. Gazing out over terracotta roof tiles, savour the moment, as soon you'll enter the forest where, for the next 7 kilometres, you'll catch only the slightest, tantalizing glimpse. Past a hotel, with 4 kilometres to go, the incline increases a little, and then, with 2 kilometres to go, a little bit more just to make sure you work hard for what is the best vantage point this side of Mont Ventoux – if it's a clear day that is!

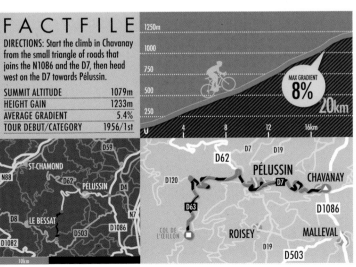

FACTFILE

DIRECTIONS: Start the climb in Chavanay from the small triangle of roads that joins the N1086 and the D7, then head west on the D7 towards Pélussin.

SUMMIT ALTITUDE	1079m
HEIGHT GAIN	1233m
AVERAGE GRADIENT	5.4%
TOUR DEBUT/CATEGORY	1956/1st

MAX GRADIENT 8%

20km

40 Col d'Entremont

There are many convoluted ways to begin this climb leaving the centre of Murat, twisting upwards through its tight and winding streets, but the chances of getting lost are high, so head west from town and start the climb on the D3 where it leaves the N122. The road climbs hard, rolls round to the right, and then sweeps left on a challenging but not overwhelming gradient under the constant gaze of the Virgin Mary standing on the peak above. The hardest climbing now behind you, circle the large roundabout and it's a straight course to the top. I've made the point of not commenting on the quality of road surfaces in this book as they are always liable to change, but here I think I must give a nod to the French road builders. Their craftsmanship is second to none, they can lay tarmac as smooth as silk, and so beautiful you want to get off the bike to stroke it. The Col d'Entremont is a perfect example of their art, so *chapeau* to the road builders of France – thank you for providing such perfect toppings for us to enjoy. Floating along, wishing my local roads were as nice, I soon arrive at the top, which lies just over a steep little brow that will force you out of the saddle to work for the end.

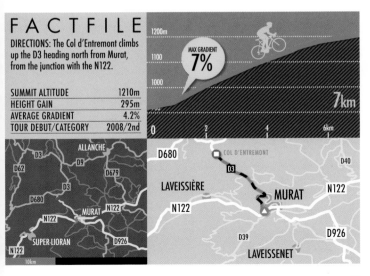

FACTFILE

DIRECTIONS: The Col d'Entremont climbs up the D3 heading north from Murat, from the junction with the N122.

SUMMIT ALTITUDE	1210m
HEIGHT GAIN	295m
AVERAGE GRADIENT	4.2%
TOUR DEBUT/CATEGORY	2008/2nd

MAX GRADIENT
7%

7km

41 Col de Prat de Bouc

Heading south from Murat, this climb's statistics mask its hidden perils. It may only have an average gradient of 5.6%, but there are a number of wicked little ramps along its route. The first bit of tough climbing comes right at the start where it kicks up across a railway line, through some buildings, across a bridge, and into woodland. It continues hard for a couple of kilometres, framed by the wooded banks, before the slope subsides significantly to almost level on the approach to the halfway point and the village of Albepierre-Bredons. Twist through the narrow streets, and then exit by banking hard left. And it's steep: 15%, bending first left then gradually right, before the gradient disperses and once more you can ride in comfort. Ticking off the kilometres you reach three to go, and up ahead you see a row of peaks in the distance that look as if they should mark the summit but are simply too far away. At a large, flat, right-hand bend, you head back on yourself, and then into a right-hand hairpin, steep round the corner to line up for the final push to the top. It's an easy finish, so put the hammer down to cross the peak at speed, at the base of the micro ski station.

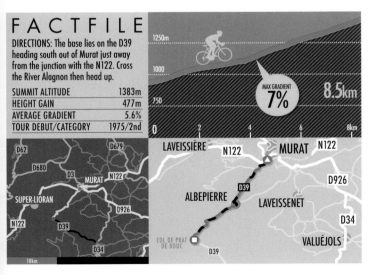

FACTFILE

DIRECTIONS: The base lies on the D39 heading south out of Murat just away from the junction with the N122. Cross the River Alagnon then head up.

SUMMIT ALTITUDE	1383m
HEIGHT GAIN	477m
AVERAGE GRADIENT	5.6%
TOUR DEBUT/CATEGORY	1975/2nd

MAX GRADIENT 7%

8.5km

1250m
1000
750
0   2   4   6   8km

D62   D679
D680   D3   MURAT   N122
SUPER-LIORAN
  D926
N122   D39
D34
10km

LAVEISSIÈRE   N122   MURAT   N122
  D39
ALBEPIERRE   D926   LAVEISSENET
COL DE PRAT DE BOUC   D34
  D39   VALUÉJOLS

42 Pas de Peyrol

In my opinion this is the best climb in the region, and what's more, there are three ways to the top: the hard, the harder, and the hardest routes. This is of course the hardest, and although significantly shorter than the other two, boy does it pack a punch – it's an absolute killer! Heading south, following a short descent you hit the base, so take your momentum into the early slopes, keep the legs spinning and make the most of the mild gradient that will do little more than soften your legs up. Once you begin to track left, crossing the double bridges, it is now that the proper climb starts – and this is a proper climb. Up next are 2 kilometres – count them, two – of solid 15% gradient, so kiss your saddle goodbye and begin to fight up this relentless, merciless incline. At halfway, around the bend, you're allowed the briefest of respite before plunging back into it once more, like a free diver breaking the surface for a mouthful of air before disappearing once more into the depths. From here it never gives in, not for a second, and with screaming legs and burning lungs, take care through the car park that lines the final metres as you drag yourself to the summit before, of course, heading off to ride the other two ascents!

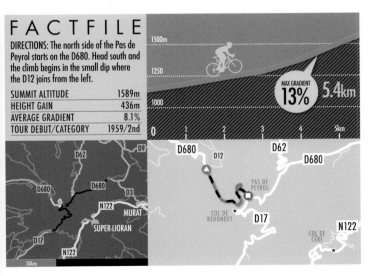

FACTFILE

DIRECTIONS: The north side of the Pas de Peyrol starts on the D680. Head south and the climb begins in the small dip where the D12 joins from the left.

SUMMIT ALTITUDE	1589m
HEIGHT GAIN	436m
AVERAGE GRADIENT	8.1%
TOUR DEBUT/CATEGORY	1959/2nd

MAX GRADIENT 13% 5.4km

43 Côte de la Croix-Neuve

The Côte de la Croix-Neuve has more recently been dubbed the Montée Laurent Jalabert after the renowned climber's emphatic solo win at the Mende Aerodrome following his attack on the climb's savage slopes in the 1995 Tour. At only 3 kilometres it's no mountain and is the shortest climb in the book, but trust me – these are three of the longest kilometres you'll ride. Leaving Mende due south on the D25, following the signs to the aerodrome, it's steep from the start; you reach a fork where you break left and then follow the road round to the right and out of town. Before you know it you've cracked the first kilometre – you're a third of the way – but don't for a minute think you're nearly there. The following kilometre, set on an average gradient of 11%, and steeper in places, succeeds in slowing all time and space. With your heart thumping and lungs burning, you crawl upwards – this road even looks steep on TV – but the way the pros dance up it beggars belief. With 2 kilometres covered, and losing the will to live, it's little comfort to know you've almost made it – but you have – and as the summit appears you have the choice to peak to the right, or to the left, following in Jalabert's wheel tracks to the aerodrome.

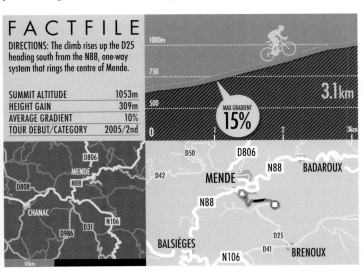

FACTFILE

DIRECTIONS: The climb rises up the D25 heading south from the N88, one-way system that rings the centre of Mende.

SUMMIT ALTITUDE	1053m
HEIGHT GAIN	309m
AVERAGE GRADIENT	10%
TOUR DEBUT/CATEGORY	2005/2nd

MAX GRADIENT
15%

3.1km

VOSGES

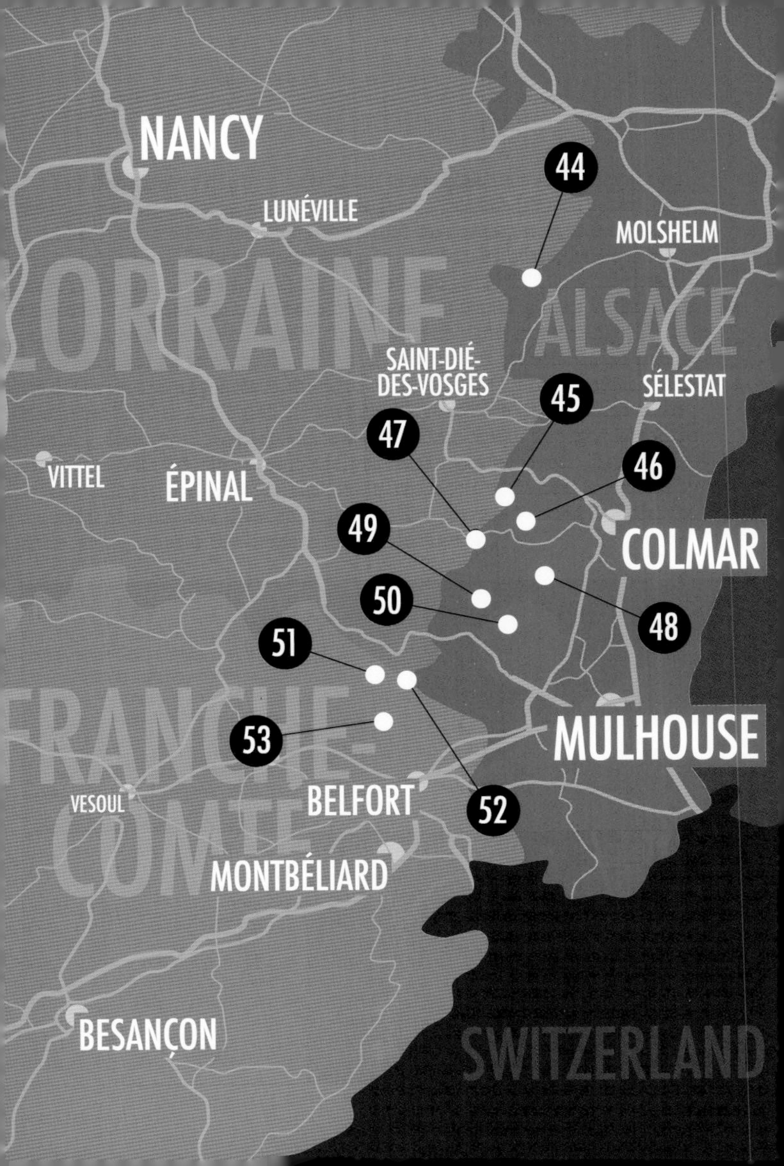

NANCY

LUNÉVILLE

MOLSHELM

LORRAINE

ALSACE

SAINT-DIÉ-
DES-VOSGES

SÉLESTAT

44

45

46

47

VITTEL

ÉPINAL

49

COLMAR

50

48

51

FRANCHE-

MULHOUSE

53

COMTÉ

VESOUL

BELFORT

52

MONTBÉLIARD

BESANÇON

SWITZERLAND

44 Col du Donon

Lying at the top edge of the Vosges, the Col du Donon is the northernmost climb in this book. It boasts, at my count, five routes to the summit. With roads leaving its peak like lava flowing from a volcano, it's hard to pick one over another – maybe you could try to ride them all in a day? The short, sharp ascent away from Raon-lès-Leau tempted me, but in the end I chose to ride the climb heading west from Schirmeck as it is the most concise and simplest route to define. Head out of town on the D392 and the slope is gentle as it meanders through the wonderfully named village of Wackenbach. It's not until the 6-kilometres-to-go point that it wakes up; you'll have to click down a few sprockets now as it touches 7%. It doesn't hold this for long, and within a kilometre drops back to a more modest 6% for the rest of your journey up through the forest. The further you climb the denser the canopy becomes, and then you reach the solitary hairpin, which forces you to dig in a little as you exit it. From here on in it's a beautiful road to ride as it twists and weaves between the trees to the clearing at the top and the junction of the many roads outside the Hotel le Velleca.

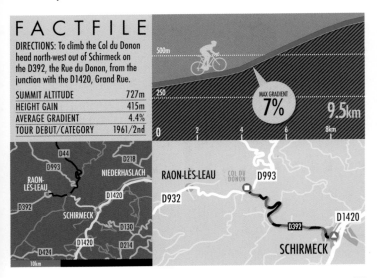

FACTFILE

DIRECTIONS: To climb the Col du Donon head north-west out of Schirmeck on the D392, the Rue du Donon, from the junction with the D1420, Grand Rue.

SUMMIT ALTITUDE	727m
HEIGHT GAIN	415m
AVERAGE GRADIENT	4.4%
TOUR DEBUT/CATEGORY	1961/2nd

MAX GRADIENT
7%

9.5km

500m

250

0   2   4   6   8km

D44
D993
D218
NIEDERHASLACH
RAON-LES-LEAU
D1420
D392
SCHIRMECK
D130
D1420
D214
D424
10km

RAON-LÈS-LEAU   COL DU DONON   D993
D932
D392   D1420
SCHIRMECK

45 Col du Calvaire

You know the saying 'the whole is greater than the sum of its parts'? Well, that's the perfect way to sum up this climb. On its own, the Col du Calvaire is a mere bump, but attack it from the village of Hachimette and you must first tackle the Col du Bonhomme and the Col du Louschbach on your way. Ridden together these three average climbs certainly create a formidable challenge. Leave Hachimette heading west on the D415 and rise gently on the wide road up to Bonhomme where it kicks up a touch through the village. It then eases back again to lead you through a tangle of bends to the first of the three peaks at the junction with the D148. Head left on to a much quieter road and up into the forest. There are no significant corners or dramatic increases in gradient, but there is a very odd peak to the Col du Louschbach. The road drops down, rounds a tight left-hand bend and there is the summit sign in the bottom of the hollow. From here the road ramps up to its steepest gradient of 8% through a couple of hairpins, and it feels like a proper mountain road for the remainder of its journey to the final of the three peaks at the junction with the D48.

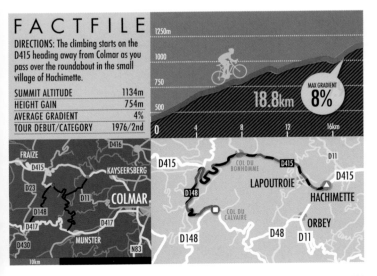

FACTFILE

DIRECTIONS: The climbing starts on the D415 heading away from Colmar as you pass over the roundabout in the small village of Hachimette.

SUMMIT ALTITUDE	1134m
HEIGHT GAIN	754m
AVERAGE GRADIENT	4%
TOUR DEBUT/CATEGORY	1976/2nd

18.8km

MAX GRADIENT 8%

46 Collet du Linge

This twisted and contorted climb rises up and away from the D417 into a wonderful series of bends – for the most part – set on a perfectly amiable 6% gradient. It's a busy climb as you pass through two protracted villages with the scenery alternating between houses, open fields, and forest. I say the gradient is generally an amiable 6%, but there are a couple of slightly tougher stretches that touch 8% although certainly no steeper. Heading through the scattered houses that collectively form the village of Hohrodberg, the hairpins are all but stacked on top of each other and it is here that you'll find the hardest slopes. Once you leave the village behind, things get easier and you climb gently through fields with a scattering of trees before plunging into typical Vosges forestland. You now have a couple of kilometres in the shadows of the tall, dark conifers, to the junction with the D11 where you take the left turn for the final short rise to the top. For those of you who know your war history, you will recognize this as the scene of a particularly bloody Second World War battle between the French and Germans; the memorials that mark the summit are a substantial tribute to those who lost their lives.

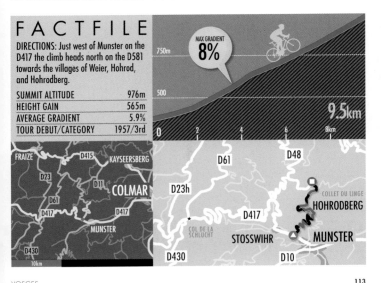

FACTFILE

DIRECTIONS: Just west of Munster on the D417 the climb heads north on the D581 towards the villages of Weier, Hohrod, and Hohrodberg.

SUMMIT ALTITUDE	976m
HEIGHT GAIN	565m
AVERAGE GRADIENT	5.9%
TOUR DEBUT/CATEGORY	1957/3rd

MAX GRADIENT **8%**

750m
500
0   2   4   6   8km
9.5km

FRAIZE   D415   KAYSEERSBERG
D23   D11   COLMAR
D61   D417
D417
MUNSTER
D430
10km

D61   D48
D23h
D417   COL DE LA SCHLUCHT
D430   STOSSWIHR   D10
COLLET DU LINGE   HOHRODBERG
MUNSTER

47 Col de la Schlucht

Let's be honest, this can be a pretty busy road, and were it not such a regular inclusion in the Tour it might not have made the cut, so avoid riding during rush hour. To start, leave the centre of Munster heading west on the D417 and up to Soultzeren, where, with 13 kilometres still to go, the gradient increases slightly. Not by much, though, just enough to warrant a gear change through the brilliant twisting bends that characterize this attractive village. Leaving Soultzeren, the now-wide road settles into its mild 5% incline and from here to the top never threatens anything more: it just ambles upwards, a stress-free ascent through picturesque grassland and thick forest. Never straight, mind – not for an inch – and with 5 kilometres to go you'll notice the scenery becoming more rugged, the road even wider, but the gradient just rolls on, the same gentle 5%. Approaching the summit, the road is framed to your right with a sheer face of bare rock and to your left with stunning views across the rolling forested peaks. Around bend after bend you arrive at the climb's signature feature where the road squeezes through a tunnel carved in the rock, before finishing amongst a rabble of slightly shabby restaurants and cafés.

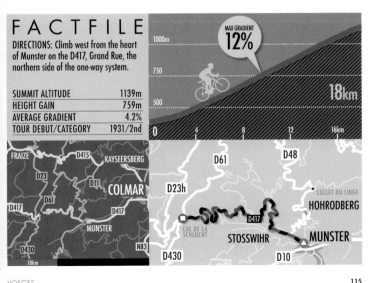

FACTFILE

DIRECTIONS: Climb west from the heart of Munster on the D417, Grand Rue, the northern side of the one-way system.

SUMMIT ALTITUDE	1139m
HEIGHT GAIN	759m
AVERAGE GRADIENT	4.2%
TOUR DEBUT/CATEGORY	1931/2nd

MAX GRADIENT
12%

18km

48 Col du Firstplan

The Col du Firstplan is the typical Vosges climb: narrow, rugged, quiet, and thickly forested. There are a handful of ways to reach the summit. I chose to start in the village of Soultzmatt where the D18 heads north, signposted 'Munster'. Rising up out of town, it's a while before you pass the last house and start the predominantly straight journey up to Osenbach. At the centre of the village the road turns into the D40 and you take the right fork, becoming steeper for a while past the beautiful houses up towards the forest. Out of town, the slope backs off before it begins to climb at a solid and consistent 6 to 7% but never steeper. Once past the last sign of settlement and agriculture, there's the junction with the D1.V where you follow the narrowing road round to the left. As you climb, the forest becomes thicker, the trees taller, and the birdsong louder. You are immersed in nature, a lone rider on a tiny road passing through the dark, pristine forest; soak in your surroundings and breathe the fresh air as you keep climbing. Weaving back and forth, through the odd hairpin, your journey to the summit comes to an end as the road crests then sweeps right.

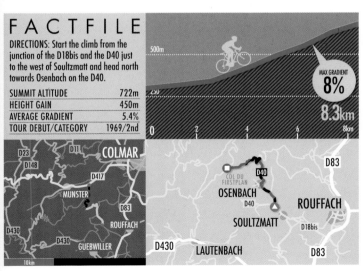

FACTFILE

DIRECTIONS: Start the climb from the junction of the D18bis and the D40 just to the west of Soultzmatt and head north towards Osenbach on the D40.

SUMMIT ALTITUDE	722m
HEIGHT GAIN	450m
AVERAGE GRADIENT	5.4%
TOUR DEBUT/CATEGORY	1969/2nd

MAX GRADIENT
8%

8.3km

49 Col du Platzerwasel

What an evil, EVIL road. I could end my description right there but I'll go on. On paper it's not the toughest climb, but in reality it's right up there. Maybe it was the persistent rain I rode in or the coarse surface, but more likely it was the steady 9% gradient. You could argue that the climb's origins are in Munster, but the action doesn't really start until you reach the town of Metzeral, so I'm calling the base outside the Hotel du Pont. Pass through town on the D10 into the next village, Sondernach; through this village the road then turns into the D27. Passing the 'Col ouvert' sign, you bank right and suddenly have to click down through gears, down, and down as you begin 6 kilometres of pure grinding. Up through the towering conifers the gradient is a punishing 9% – closer to 10% – there's a long straight, followed by a tangle of bends followed by a long straight, and this repeats for the remainder of the climb. The bends are blessed relief from your toil but do nothing to help you reach the end. You force your way up to the summit sign, but annoyingly it's not the top: you have one more effort to round the next corner before you've conquered this hidden beast of the Vosges.

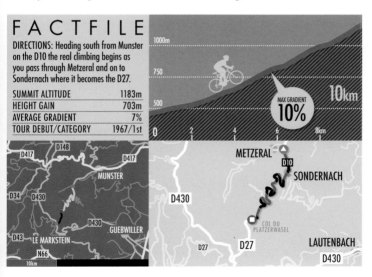

FACTFILE

DIRECTIONS: Heading south from Munster on the D10 the real climbing begins as you pass through Metzeral and on to Sondernach where it becomes the D27.

SUMMIT ALTITUDE	1183m
HEIGHT GAIN	703m
AVERAGE GRADIENT	7%
TOUR DEBUT/CATEGORY	1967/1st

MAX GRADIENT 10%

10km

50 Grand Ballon

Leaving Willer-sur-Thur, in the far distance you'll catch sight of the giant radar that sits on top of the Grand Ballon, its white dome shining like a beacon, calling all cyclists to the top of the highest point in the Vosges. The first 2 kilometres are gentle, and then the next 4 kilometres a little tougher but nothing more than 6% up to the village of Goldbach-Altenbach. Here there's a dip, followed by more of the benign gradient, which brings you to the junction with the D431 and the summit of the Col d'Amic. Swing left and the climbing changes abruptly, click down a few sprockets and soon you find yourself at the first of two quite unique stretches of road. As you approach the corner, you double take – PAVÉ! Out of nowhere the sweep of the bend, just 20m, is covered with Belgium's finest! Rumble round and a couple of hundred metres up the road there is another short stretch to rob you of a little more momentum. Exiting the forest, the slope kicks up to a substantial 8%, and as you enter the open grassland you catch your first sight of the radar since you set off. These last 3 kilometres are tough, but the views are stunning as you cross the grassy peaks to summit on the small plateau.

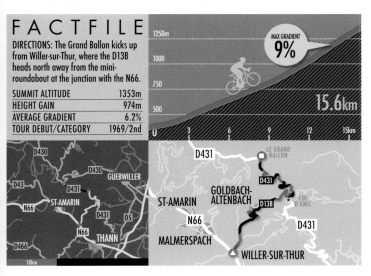

FACTFILE

DIRECTIONS: The Grand Ballon kicks up from Willer-sur-Thur, where the D13B heads north away from the mini-roundabout at the junction with the N66.

SUMMIT ALTITUDE	1353m
HEIGHT GAIN	974m
AVERAGE GRADIENT	6.2%
TOUR DEBUT/CATEGORY	1969/2nd

MAX GRADIENT
9%

15.6km

1250m
1000
750
500

0   3   6   9   12   15km

51 Ballon d'Alsace

As you sit at the base of the Ballon d'Alsace, brace yourself for 9 kilometres of pure climbing joy. Leave Saint-Maurice-sur-Moselle and you're straight into a tangle of switchbacks; for 2 kilometres the bends are frequent and the corners steep, forcing you from your saddle to preserve momentum. Once free from its chaotic start, the climb makes its way through meadows and farmland before entering forest. Now hidden in the trees the bends return, but this time the corners are far less abrupt and the distance between bends much longer. Each one arrives just when you need one, although the gradient is pretty much a constant 6 to 7%, and when a certain stretch begins to drag a little, a corner arrives to refresh the legs and you leave rejuvenated to begin the next. This perfect frequency of bend–straight–bend will allow you to tick off the kilometres with ease as you exit the forest, riding through an immaculate open meadow thick with mountain flowers before lining up for the push to the summit. Just 1,500m of all but dead-straight climbing lie ahead up to the distinctive brow and the finish amongst a collection of cafés and souvenir shops.

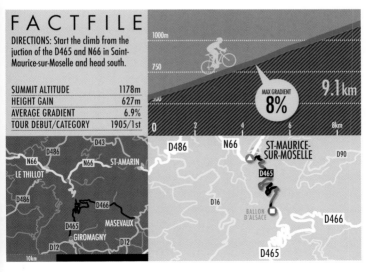

FACTFILE

DIRECTIONS: Start the climb from the juction of the D465 and N66 in Saint-Maurice-sur-Moselle and head south.

SUMMIT ALTITUDE	1178m
HEIGHT GAIN	627m
AVERAGE GRADIENT	6.9%
TOUR DEBUT/CATEGORY	1905/1st

MAX GRADIENT
8%

9.1km

52 Ballon de Servance

If your legs scream in the forest and no one is around to hear them, do they really hurt? Well, you'll soon find out. The Ballon de Servance is a lonely, rugged and extremely tough climb that lies hidden in thick forest, like a hunter's trap waiting to snare unsuspecting riders. Head up out of Plancher-Bas, north through the valley, and the road seems for all the world to be flat, but on inspection of the profile, yes, you are climbing. For each passing kilometre you'll gain just a few metres in height, but once through Plancher-les-Mines things start to change. First of all there's a tiny 20% ramp, which stuns the legs into activity, followed shortly after by the split in the road that leads up to the Planche des Belles Filles. Bear left at the junction and the road begins to step upwards. You'll be lucky to see a single soul this far up the climb, which is good as they won't witness how you suffer once you reach the left-hand hairpin that launches you into 3 kilometres of 8 and 9% climbing. This serious escalation in the gradient is not to be underestimated, and it provides a tough and prolonged finale to what started out as such a placid climb.

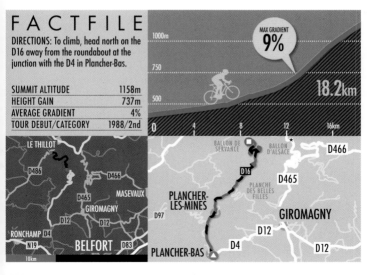

FACTFILE

DIRECTIONS: To climb, head north on the D16 away from the roundabout at the junction with the D4 in Plancher-Bas.

SUMMIT ALTITUDE	1158m
HEIGHT GAIN	737m
AVERAGE GRADIENT	4%
TOUR DEBUT/CATEGORY	1988/2nd

MAX GRADIENT
9%

1000m
750
500

18.2km

0   4   8   12   16km

53 Planche des Belles Filles

There's been a trend recently in the three 'Grand Tours' to supplement the usual mountain passes with much shorter and steeper climbs. Usually placed at the end of the stages, they present a brutal challenge to the riders but create fantastic drama for the spectators. One such climb is the Planche des Belles Filles. Begin as the D16A splits from the D16 and – OUCH! Right away it's steep, and it only gets worse. Within the first kilometre it ramps up to 13%, until reaching a slight brow, and then the gradient drops to a manageable 7% and even briefly levels before it hits you again – BANG – another vicious ramp attacks your legs, 10%, then 12% then back to 10%. Just imagine racing this beast with 200 kilometres in your legs – it's unthinkable. Mercifully, it's short and after just 5 kilometres of climbing, following a slight respite, you line up to tackle the finale. Specially extended for the 2012 Tour, this 20% ramp of fresh tarmac will have you weaving from left to right, heaving each pedal over the next to reach the summit. Ahead lies the finishing line and next to it a sign telling you that Britain's Chris Froome climbed it in just 16 minutes, 11 seconds. You look down at your computer and then look up again, shaking your head in disbelief.

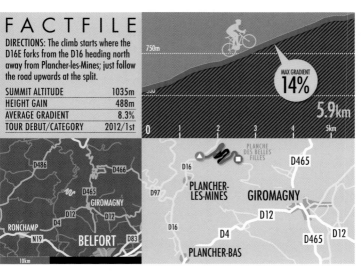

FACTFILE

DIRECTIONS: The climb starts where the D16E forks from the D16 heading north away from Plancher-les-Mines; just follow the road upwards at the split.

SUMMIT ALTITUDE	1035m
HEIGHT GAIN	488m
AVERAGE GRADIENT	8.3%
TOUR DEBUT/CATEGORY	2012/1st

MAX GRADIENT
14%

5.9km

750m

0   1   2   3   4   5km

D486
D466
D465
GIROMAGNY
D12
D12
D4
RONCHAMP
N19
BELFORT
D83
10km

D16
PLANCHE DES BELLES FILLES
D465
D97
PLANCHER-LES-MINES
GIROMAGNY
D12
D16
D4
D465
D12
PLANCHER-BAS

THE SPECTATOR'S GUIDE

TO A DAY IN THE MOUNTAINS

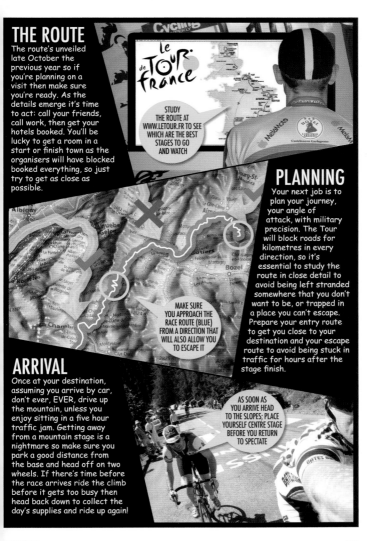

THE ROUTE

The route's unveiled late October the previous year so if you're planning on a visit then make sure you're ready. As the details emerge it's time to act: call your friends, call work, then get your hotels booked. You'll be lucky to get a room in a start or finish town as the organisers will have blocked booked everything, so just try to get as close as possible.

> STUDY THE ROUTE AT WWW.LETOUR.FR TO SEE WHICH ARE THE BEST STAGES TO GO AND WATCH

PLANNING

Your next job is to plan your journey, your angle of attack, with military precision. The Tour will block roads for kilometres in every direction, so it's essential to study the route in close detail to avoid being left stranded somewhere that you don't want to be, or trapped in a place you can't escape. Prepare your entry route to get you close to your destination and your escape route to avoid being stuck in traffic for hours after the stage finish.

> MAKE SURE YOU APPROACH THE RACE ROUTE (BLUE) FROM A DIRECTION THAT WILL ALSO ALLOW YOU TO ESCAPE IT

ARRIVAL

Once at your destination, assuming you arrive by car, don't ever, EVER, drive up the mountain, unless you enjoy sitting in a five hour traffic jam. Getting away from a mountain stage is a nightmare so make sure you park a good distance from the base and head off on two wheels. If there's time before the race arrives ride the climb before it gets too busy then head back down to collect the day's supplies and ride up again!

> AS SOON AS YOU ARRIVE HEAD TO THE SLOPES; PLACE YOURSELF CENTRE STAGE BEFORE YOU RETURN TO SPECTATE

WHAT TO PACK

Here's a list of the ESSENTIALS to pack to enjoy a perfect day on a mountain. Of course the amount of stuff you take is limited to what you can carry, though! 1 Flags, 2 Beer, 3 Spare jacket, 4 Quality umbrella, 5 Newspaper, 6 Large sign, 7 Camera, 8 Chalk, 9 Knife, 10 Electrical tape, 11 Water, 12 Sunscreen, 13 Saucisson, 14 Bread, 15 Cheese.

> TRY TO FIND A VANTAGE POINT WHERE YOU CAN SEE THE RACE CLIMB UP THROUGH THE VALLEY

> STAND CLOSE TO A KILOMETRE MARKER TO MAXIMIZE YOUR CHANCES OF BEING SPOTTED ON TV!

PICKING A SPOT

Bags packed, it's time to find a good place to stand, and you MUST arrive over an hour before the publicity caravan to avoid the firm hand of a gendarme halting your progress. There are three key ingredients to look for in a location:
1 a view down the valley to track the race.
2 a long line of sight when it gets close, and 3 next to a landmark that will be on TV.

> STUDY THE ROAD, TRY TO STAND ON THE SIDE YOU WOULD EXPECT THE RIDERS TO USE TO GET AS CLOSE AS POSSIBLE

THE CARAVAN

The first rule of the publicity caravan is that there are no rules. Preceding the race along the entirety of its route, cheery young people fling everything from hats to sausages at you from a multitude of bizarre vehicles. For 30 minutes, the population of France turn to feral beasts as they push and fight for all manner of useless tat. Mark your territory, weigh up your rivals, and prepare to do battle.

NO MATTER WHAT FLIES THROUGH THE AIR, IT'S ALL TREASURE AND YOU MUST FIGHT FOR EVERY LAST ITEM

THIS IS YOUR TERRITORY. GUARD IT WELL, ALLOW NO MAN OR WOMAN TO ENTER, LET ALONE GRAB ANYTHING OUT

BE PREPARED TO SEE ANYTHING FROM A GIANT CHEESE ON WHEELS TO A MOTORIZED CROISSANT

NO MATTER HOW INSIGNIFICANT, CHASE EVERY ITEM, EVEN IF IT MEANS JUMPING INTO A STREAM OR MUDDY FIELD

I've had kids pushing me into ditches and old women stamping on my hands, all for the prize a 25g bag of Haribo, it's a feverish environment, so here are a couple of tips to help you. If you're in a group, spread out to cover more ground and keep your hands empty so it appears you've caught nothing. The key tip is to stand close but not too close to children. Essentially you are using them as bait but with your superior height you will be able to intercept goodies before they reach them. Be warned, though, it's wise to offer up a few items when you have spares to keep their parents happy.

RELAX

Now that the caravan's passed you'll have a good hour to wait till the race arrives so sit back, have a beer, eat some cheese, and admire the bounty of rubbish, I mean treasure, you've just acquired. Keep your ears open, though, listening for the faint sound of helicopter blades. Nothing compares to that first sound of the beating rotors as this means the race is finally coming!

THE SKY FILLS WITH HELICOPTERS FILMING THE RACE AND BOUNCING THE TV SIGNALS BACK TO SATELLITES

WHETHER YOU READ FRENCH OR NOT TRY TO BLEND IN BY STUDYING THE RESULTS IN THAT DAY'S COPY OF L'EQUIPE

WAVE A DISTINCTIVE SIGN SO YOU CAN SPOT YOURSELF ON THE RACE FOOTAGE THAT YOU'RE RECORDING BACK HOME

IF YOU DON'T WANT TO CARRY A LITRE OF PAINT UP A MOUNTAIN, YOU CAN SCRAWL YOUR SUPPORT ON A FLAG

THE RACE

Now it's action time. Depending on the stretch of the peloton it could all be over in seconds, so you have to decide what you'll do when it arrives. Do you wave a sign? Take photos? Scream at the riders to ALLEZ! ALLEZ! Or simply soak it all in as your idols pass in a blur of sweat and colour, their legs cut from mahogany, screaming with the effort.

PHOTOS

If you do decide to capture the race with your camera, then unless you're very well practised or have professional equipment, prepare for many disappointments. Like sifting through a pan of silt, though, every now and again you'll find a nugget of gold – that killer shot to remember your day by.

PREPARE FOR MOST OF YOUR SHOTS TO COME OUT LIKE THIS, BUT YOU MIGHT GET LUCKY LIKE I DID ABOVE

TV

Back home, your relatives will be glued to the nightly highlights, or even the live coverage, not interested in the racing but in waiting to catch the slightest glimpse of you on the screen. So if you want them to spot you, you'll need to stand out in the crowd, but do remember that you're just the background; do NOT interfere with the race, it isn't about YOU after all.

NO! THAT'S NOT DADDY RIDING HIS BIKE, DADDY'S THE ONE SCREAMING AND WAVING THE SIGN!

MOVE ON

As soon as the last vehicle's passed it's time to head off, so be packed and ready to join the crowds hurtling down to the base to do it all over again on another mountain. Make sure you take all your litter because for the other 364 days of the year the spot where you've spent the day is pristine countryside and that's the way it should stay. Oh, apart from the paint on the road that is!

A LASTING LEGACY OF THE TOUR, THE PAINT ON THE ROAD BECOMES A PERMANENT PART OF THE SCENERY

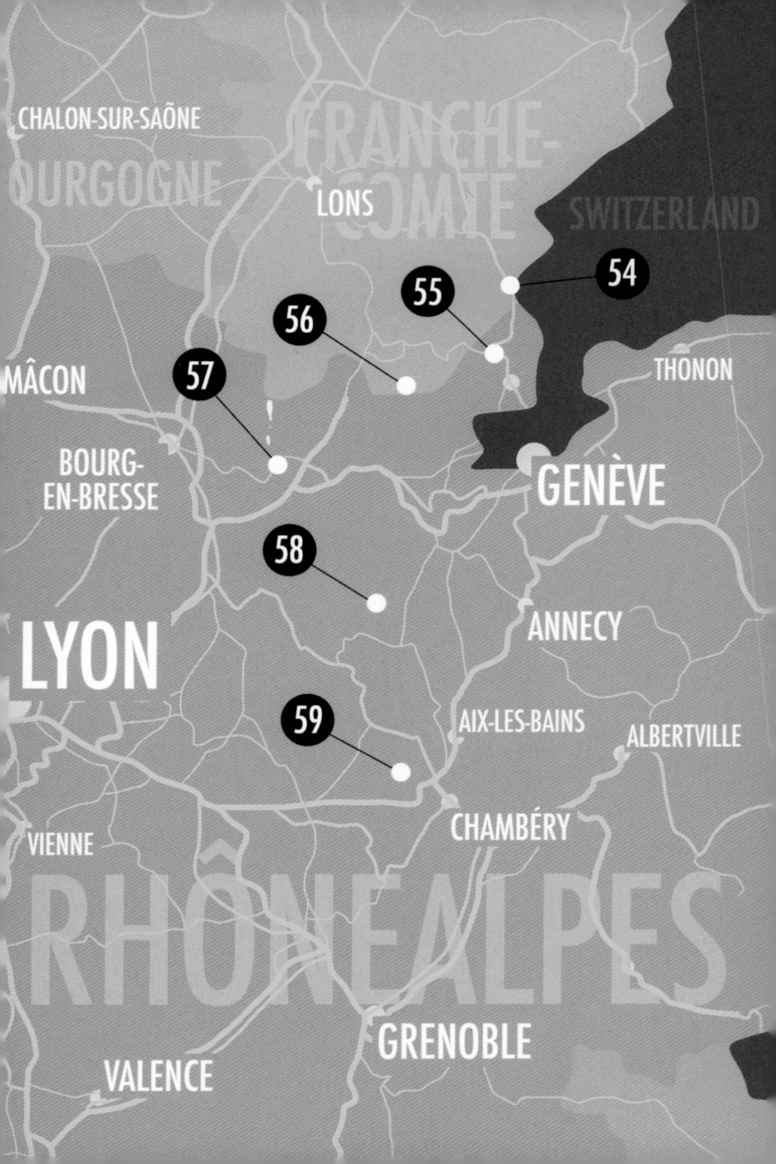
CHALON-SUR-SAÔNE
OURGOGNE
FRANCHE-COMTE
LONS
SWITZERLAND
54
55
56
57
MÂCON
THONON
BOURG-EN-BRESSE
GENÈVE
58
ANNECY
LYON
59
AIX-LES-BAINS
ALBERTVILLE
CHAMBÉRY
VIENNE
RHÔNEALPES
GRENOBLE
VALENCE

54 Côte des Rousses

The Côte des Rousses is in many ways an unremarkable climb, but it's one that has seen a surprising amount of Tour action since its debut in 1967. Over the years, riders come and go, trees grow, houses are built, but the roads – their topography, corners, ups and downs – they stay the same. They are a constant, a stage that is set 365 days of the year just waiting for a fresh set of actors, be they pro riders or weekend warriors, willing to do battle on them. You start this particular 'scene' in the town of Morez; exit on the N5, which can be busy at times, and simply follow it all the way to the top. Heading due south to begin, the road soon starts to bend, winding up through the conifered hillsides and exquisite grassy meadows. If you arrive at the bottom with good legs then you really can attack this climb; the mild-mannered gradient never rears up enough to cause you any real discomfort and allows you to maintain a constant speed from base to summit. On the final approach to Rousses the road widens, lined either side with a plethora of advertising hoardings and road furniture; bending right, into the centre of town, as the slope fades away, the climb finishes on the plateau.

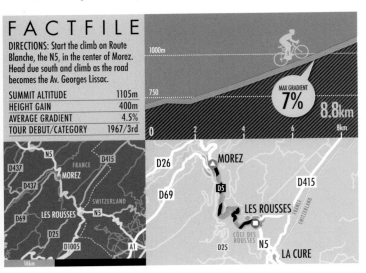

FACTFILE

DIRECTIONS: Start the climb on Route Blanche, the N5, in the center of Morez. Head due south and climb as the road becomes the Av. Georges Lissac.

SUMMIT ALTITUDE	1105m
HEIGHT GAIN	400m
AVERAGE GRADIENT	4.5%
TOUR DEBUT/CATEGORY	1967/3rd

MAX GRADIENT
7%

8.8km

1000m

750

0 2 4 6 8km

N5
D437
D415
FRANCE
MOREZ
D437
SWITZERLAND
LES ROUSSES N5
D69
D25
D1005 A1
10km

D26
MOREZ
D5
D415
D69
LES ROUSSES
FRANCE
SWITZERLAND
CÔTE DES
ROUSSES
D25 N5
LA CURE

55 Col de la Faucille

If you're only going to ride one mountain in the Jura, make sure it's this one; I guarantee you will not be disappointed – it's fantastic. Heading out of the beautiful town of Gex, the early slopes are nice and gentle as you pick your way through the streets heading into the Jura National Park. No one likes to start a climb on a vicious ramp, it ruins the legs, and so an affable introduction is always welcome. Don't get over excited though – you'd be wise to keep plenty in the tank for what lies further ahead, so spin the gears. At roughly 6 kilometres along, take the opportunity to look over your left shoulder to drink in the stunning view of the vast plain disappearing into the distance. Savour this moment because it's not long before the hard work starts; rounding an abandoned house at the apex of a left-hand hairpin, the gradient ramps up significantly. Up until now the kilometres have been flying by with relative ease, but from now on you'll feel like you're stuck in quicksand. With 10 kilometres under your belt, you reach an enormous hairpin that leads you into the last twists and turns to the top. Up ahead there's a brow – it's not the summit, but it acts as a springboard – cross it, dip down then burst out of the saddle to force a sprint to finish on the plateau.

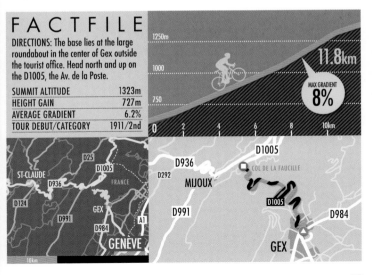

FACTFILE

DIRECTIONS: The base lies at the large roundabout in the center of Gex outside the tourist office. Head north and up on the D1005, the Av. de la Poste.

SUMMIT ALTITUDE	1323m
HEIGHT GAIN	727m
AVERAGE GRADIENT	6.2%
TOUR DEBUT/CATEGORY	1911/2nd

11.8km

MAX GRADIENT
8%

56 Col de la Croix de la Serra

The Col de la Croix de la Serra kicks off just outside Saint-Claude where the D124 splits from the D436 at the 90-degree corner in Rochefort. The gradient is mild, permanently mild. There are a handful of gentle curves but no hairpins, and certainly no punishing ramps to force you from your saddle. You can settle into a rhythm almost straight away and begin to tick methodically over the kilometres as you creep gently up the side of the valley. As you rise, make sure you take in the perfect chocolate-box scenery all around you: the tiny villages of neat alpine houses occupying the oases of perfectly manicured grassland that punctuate the neatly conifered slopes. It's simply a joy to ride through such immaculate surroundings. Once you've covered 8 kilometres, there's a significant plateau and slight dip, and although it's not been a grind up to this point it is still a welcome break to refresh the legs. The hiatus lasts roughly a kilometre then it's back into the climb and the push for the top. The last stretch gets gradually easier, and you're free to click up the gears as the small white cross that marks the summit of this stunningly beautiful road comes into view.

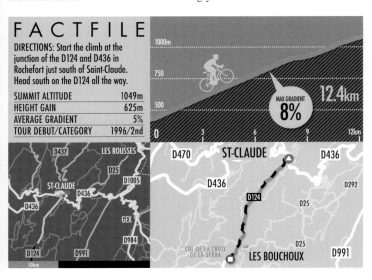

FACTFILE

DIRECTIONS: Start the climb at the junction of the D124 and D436 in Rochefort just south of Saint-Claude. Head south on the D124 all the way.

SUMMIT ALTITUDE	1049m
HEIGHT GAIN	625m
AVERAGE GRADIENT	5%
TOUR DEBUT/CATEGORY	1996/2nd

MAX GRADIENT 8%

12.4km

57 Col du Berthiand

The Col du Berthiand is a transitional climb, situated on the western edge of the Jura, and it's included on routes leading the riders towards or away from the Alps. Begin as you descend from Hautecourt-Romanèche on the D91 heading east across the Pont de Serrières-sur-Ain. Once over the river you hit the slope right away and – BANG – the solid gradient is a real shock to the legs. Passing the battered and faded sign that hopefully proclaims the 'Col ouvert', the wide but quiet road ramps up to a touch over 10%. The toughest climbing is found on these early slopes as you force your way up to a brace of sweeping bends both as steep as the stretch that preceded them. The gradient then recedes as you exit the bends and rise dead straight for a couple of kilometres to a parking place on your left. This has the feel of a summit, but although the hardest climbing is behind you, you're still only about half way to the top. Next, the road bends right and eases significantly before banking left into woods and up to the climb's solitary hairpin. Sweep right, back on yourself, and then you begin to track round to the left heading to a brow in the road, but it's not quite the peak. You must travel a few hundred metres more to be rewarded with the summit sign.

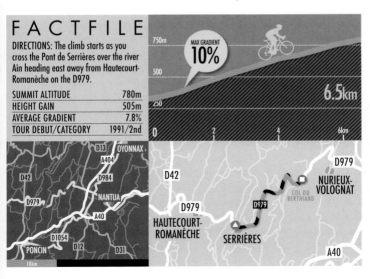

FACTFILE

DIRECTIONS: The climb starts as you cross the Pont de Serrières over the river Ain heading east away from Hautecourt-Romanèche on the D979.

SUMMIT ALTITUDE	780m
HEIGHT GAIN	505m
AVERAGE GRADIENT	7.8%
TOUR DEBUT/CATEGORY	1991/2nd

MAX GRADIENT **10%**

6.5km

58 Col du Grand Colombier

Let's cut to the chase. This climb is all about the magical set of hairpins at one-third distance; not that there's anything wrong with the rest of it, it's just that those bends, and the views they offer both rider and spectator, are simply stunning. A recent addition to the Tour's repertoire in 2012, you begin by winding up through Culoz. On the outskirts of town the road narrows and it's tough going on an 8 to 9% slope for a few kilometres. Once high above the valley, you arrive at arguably the most picture-perfect set of bends in the whole of France – so tightly packed, stacked one on top of the other, it's as if you're riding through the very intestines of the mountain. Twisting back and forth, left and right, you'll exit exhilarated but the fun ends abruptly as the road straightens and the slope ramps up to 10%. Grind through a couple of kilometres and you're rewarded with a stretch of shallow gradient to the point where the road splits. Bear left, steep up through the forest, and then, with 4 kilometres to go, the forest canopy recedes as you cross a cattle grid into open land. As you head for the summit, look for the giant cross poking over the horizon, which signals you're almost there – just one vast sweeping left-hander and you've made it.

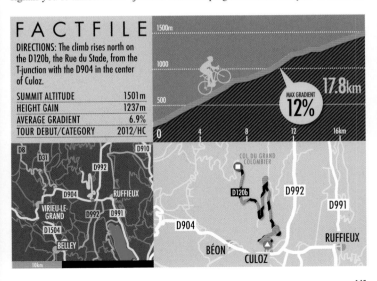

FACTFILE

DIRECTIONS: The climb rises north on the D120b, the Rue du Stade, from the T-junction with the D904 in the center of Culoz.

SUMMIT ALTITUDE	1501m
HEIGHT GAIN	1237m
AVERAGE GRADIENT	6.9%
TOUR DEBUT/CATEGORY	2012/HC

MAX GRADIENT **12%**

17.8km

59 Mont du Chat

There are few climbs as imposing as the Mont du Chat. As you stand in its shadow in Le Bourget-du-Lac, the thickly forested wall of a mountain fills the horizon like a massed army. Used only once in the Tour in 1974, it is just 2 kilometres bottom to top as the crow flies but to ride it is 13 kilometres, 13 of the toughest kilometres in the whole of France. Almost from the very start, as you head west out of town, the gradient is a constant 10%: it never backs off, never offers any help, the only respite a few metres of flat at the apex of the far too infrequent corners. Neither is there any view. You are shrouded in thick forest the entire way up; all there is to occupy you is the punishing gradient under your wheels. So relentless in its uniformity that you become acutely aware of even the slightest change, the merest alteration in the grade of the shadow on the road signifying that the slope has either risen or dipped by a fraction of a per cent. With the passing of each and every kilometre you rise another 100m back and forth from corner to corner until at last a radio mast comes into view. And there, with no fanfare, is the summit and thankfully a break in the trees allowing you a very, very hard-earned view of the fantastic lake below.

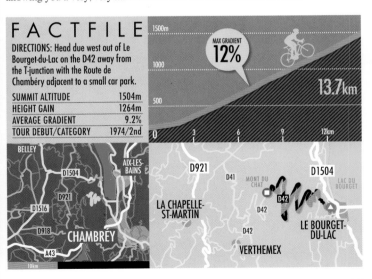

FACTFILE

DIRECTIONS: Head due west out of Le Bourget-du-Lac on the D42 away from the T-junction with the Route de Chambéry adjacent to a small car park.

SUMMIT ALTITUDE	1504m
HEIGHT GAIN	1264m
AVERAGE GRADIENT	9.2%
TOUR DEBUT/CATEGORY	1974/2nd

MAX GRADIENT
12%

13.7km

1500m
1000
500
0 · 3 · 6 · 9 · 12km

BELLEY
AIX-LES-BAINS
D1504
D921
D1516
D918
CHAMBÉRY
A43
10km

D921
D41
MONT DU CHAT
D1504
LAC DU BOURGET
LA CHAPELLE-ST-MARTIN
D42
D42
D42
LE BOURGET-DU-LAC
VERTHEMEX

ALPES
DU NORD

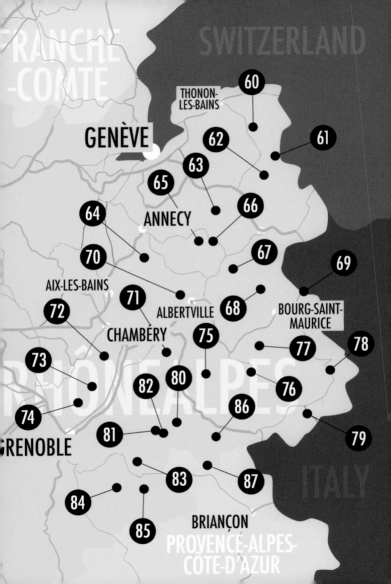

60 Col du Corbier

The northernmost of the Alpine climbs for this book is little more than a bump compared with the giants further south – the Col du Corbier has been a regular inclusion on the Tour since 1975. Lying midway between Thonon-les-Bains and Morzine, connecting the D902 and the D22, this route heads east up through the village of Le Biot. The climb starts abruptly as the D332 rises away from the main road, up and round to the right on a hard 9% slope. It gets harder – as steep as 11% – as the road twists its way into the village where you're granted a few hundred metres respite. Passing through the small collection of houses, it's straight into more 9% gradient, which once again turns into 11% before relenting. This scenario of hard, then harder, climbing plays out for a third time before the top, only on this occasion it is more protracted. You spend longer on the 9%, and even longer on the wicked 11%, before entering the final kilometre, which fades, delivering you to the summit at the Station de Drouzin le Mont. It may only be 6 kilometres long, but this climb is to be treated with respect – attack it too hard at the base and it will bite back, in more than one place.

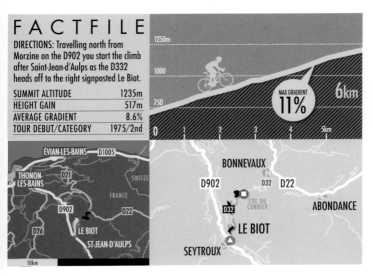

FACTFILE

DIRECTIONS: Travelling north from Morzine on the D902 you start the climb after Saint-Jean-d'Aulps as the D332 heads off to the right signposted Le Biot.

SUMMIT ALTITUDE	1235m
HEIGHT GAIN	517m
AVERAGE GRADIENT	8.6%
TOUR DEBUT/CATEGORY	1975/2nd

MAX GRADIENT 11%

6km

61 Avoriaz

Morzine is a town that bursts with adrenaline junkies twelve months of the year, and all are here to ride up, race down or simply to jump right off the mountain above. No matter what your persuasion, if you like action and adventure you'll find it, and for us road cyclists that comes in the shape of the wonderful 14-kilometre climb up to Avoriaz. Leave the eastern edge of town and above you, far in the distance, teetering on the edge of the sheer rock face, stand the resort's hotels like giant sentinels keeping watch over the valley below. Head into the forest and begin 10 kilometres of twists and turns; the gradient is a manageable 7% as you head back and forth under the ski lift carrying 'lazy' mountain bikers to their various drop-off points. With 5 kilometres to go, you leave the trees behind and the huge hotels reappear, looking for all the world like man-made extensions of the rock face. The road is now straight, and the gradient is the same 7% but this stretch is a real drag: you have a clear view of the summit, you keep pedalling but it just won't get any closer. With 1.3 kilometres to go, you pass a café and then you have the final push into Avoriaz where you can take a look back at the astonishing view of Morzine at the base of a perfect V-shaped valley.

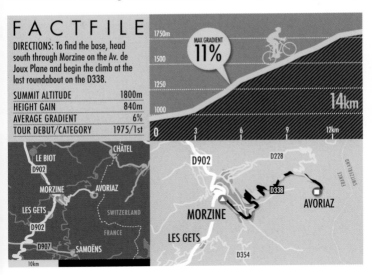

FACTFILE

DIRECTIONS: To find the base, head south through Morzine on the Av. de Joux Plane and begin the climb at the last roundabout on the D338.

SUMMIT ALTITUDE	1800m
HEIGHT GAIN	840m
AVERAGE GRADIENT	6%
TOUR DEBUT/CATEGORY	1975/1st

MAX GRADIENT **11%**

1750m
1500m
1250m
1000m

14km

0   3   6   9   12km

LE BIOT
D902
CHÂTEL
MORZINE
AVORIAZ
LES GETS
D902
SWITZERLAND
D907
FRANCE
SAMOËNS
10km

D902
D228
MORZINE
D338
AVORIAZ
FRANCE
SWITZERLAND
LES GETS
D354

62 Col de Joux Plane

Let's not beat about the bush, the Col de la Joux Plane is one hell of a tough climb with virtually the whole ride set on a 9 to 12% gradient. More Pyrenean than Alpine, its ferocious slopes and punishing hairpins will test your legs, lungs, and willpower to their limits. There are two ways to begin the climb out of Samoëns: the conventional D354, and then the one you'll ride – the Voie Communale No5. This is a vicious kilometre of narrow tarmac that doesn't just leave town – it punches its way out, draining your legs right from the get-go. When you join the D354, with 10.5 kilometres to ride you're straight into more savage climbing, first crossing agricultural land, and then with 6 kilometres to go you enter forest. OUCH, the slope hits 10% once more. The woodland's not thick, but it will offer you some protection as you toil away below its canopy. When you exit, the entire last kilometre is lined out in front of you, and there at the top you see a cluster of red umbrellas – a beacon of refreshment shimmering in the sun like an oasis in a desert. This is your goal. Push on up the gruelling final few metres to claim your reward: an ice-cold drink and the heart-stopping views of the valley below.

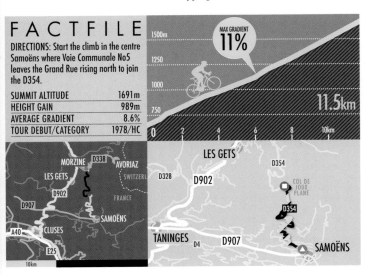

FACTFILE

DIRECTIONS: Start the climb in the centre Samoëns where Voie Communale No5 leaves the Grand Rue rising north to join the D354.

SUMMIT ALTITUDE	1691m
HEIGHT GAIN	989m
AVERAGE GRADIENT	8.6%
TOUR DEBUT/CATEGORY	1978/HC

MAX GRADIENT
11%

11.5km

63 Col de la Colombière

When I search my earliest memories of the Tour, before I was truly hooked, it is this climb that always comes to mind. Maybe though, that's got more to do with the fact that the coffee company Cafe de Colombia used to sponsor the King of the Mountains prize with a large banner at the top of each and every climb. Anyway, on leaving Scionzier via the roundabout with giant cogs on it, ahead of you stands a wall of mountains through which you must find a way. The first couple of kilometres are a breeze, and then, as you switch back on yourself, the slope creeps up to a steady 8% for a while before easing again on the approach to Le Reposoir. With its picture-postcard houses dotted around the perfectly manicured grassland, you will not ride through a more ideal Alpine village. Climb steeply out, up through a cluster of hairpins, and then it's hard going for five solid kilometres at 9%. Through forest at first then leaving the trees behind, the road starts to hug the side of the mountain. With a jagged rock face to your right and a sheer drop to your left, the final 10% kilometre is the toughest of the whole climb; grind your way to the top where there's no plateau, just the drop straight down the other side.

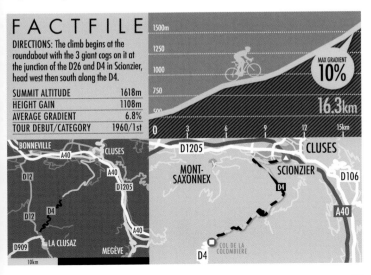

FACTFILE

DIRECTIONS: The climb begins at the roundabout with the 3 giant cogs on it at the junction of the D26 and D4 in Scionzier, head west then south along the D4.

SUMMIT ALTITUDE	1618m
HEIGHT GAIN	1108m
AVERAGE GRADIENT	6.8%
TOUR DEBUT/CATEGORY	1960/1st

MAX GRADIENT
10%

16.3km

64 Semnoz

The mountain of Le Semnoz lies to the south of Annecy and you can pick one of four paths to the summit at the Crêt de Châtillon; the most direct route heads due south out of town. To begin, find the base of the D41 and, lying ahead of you, are 17.4 kilometres of hard work to the small ski station that sits on the very peak of the mountain. Starting with four stiff kilometres of twisting back and forth through thick woodland on a 7% gradient, and then with 12 kilometres to climb, it backs off to just 3% for three very gentle kilometres. Leaving the last of a collection of large clearings, it's back into thick forest, and with 10 kilometres to go there's a vicious ramp to shock you out of any complacency that might have set in. From now on there's no chance to rest and the next 4 kilometres feature stretches of 9% climbing that will hurt the legs, but you're rewarded with amazing views through the gaps in the trees. The higher you climb, the better the sights and it's impossible not to stop to soak it all in on the way to the rugged upper slopes. The toughest is left till the end. The road begins to weave free of the forest and around rocky outcrops to finish high above the beautiful town of Annecy.

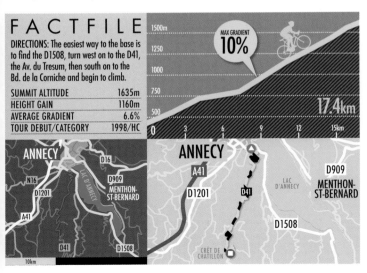

FACTFILE

DIRECTIONS: The easiest way to the base is to find the D1508, turn west on to the D41, the Av. du Tresum, then south on to the Bd. de la Corniche and begin to climb.

SUMMIT ALTITUDE	1635m
HEIGHT GAIN	1160m
AVERAGE GRADIENT	6.6%
TOUR DEBUT/CATEGORY	1998/HC

MAX GRADIENT
10%

1500m
1250
1000
750
500

17.4km

0   3   6   9   12   15km

ANNECY
D16
LAC D'ANNECY
N16
D909
MENTHON-ST-BERNARD
D1201
A41
D41   D1508
10km

ANNECY
A41
D1201   D41
LAC D'ANNECY
D909
MENTHON-ST-BERNARD
D1508
CRÊT DE CHÂTILLON

65 Col de la Croix-Fry

Forming the quiet back route between Thônes and La Clusaz, the Col de la Croix-Fry has only been used in the Tour a couple of times, which is hard to understand as it is such a great climb to ride. Leaving Thônes, the slope kicks up the moment you hit the D16: not too harsh at just over 6% to begin with, but, following a slight dip, it notches up to over 7% on the approach to Manigod. Heading into the village, the gradient vanishes and the road levels. It's tempting to stick it in the big ring here but show caution, you are far from the top – burn too many matches now and you'll be sorry. Sure enough, leaving the village, things turn nasty – BOOM – it's steep, ramping up to over 9% for two solid kilometres that will render your saddle redundant as you force the bike upwards. When you reach the point where you can't handle the slope for an inch longer, it abates and you can sit back down to tick off the kilometres with a little more ease. As you reach one to go, there's a slight pause, just long enough for you to gather yourself, and then it's the push to the summit, through a pair of beautiful hairpins, and the slope gradually fades to end amongst gift shops and restaurants.

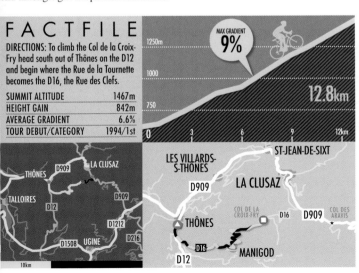

FACTFILE

DIRECTIONS: To climb the Col de la Croix-Fry head south out of Thônes on the D12 and begin where the Rue de la Tournette becomes the D16, the Rue des Clefs.

SUMMIT ALTITUDE	1467m
HEIGHT GAIN	842m
AVERAGE GRADIENT	6.6%
TOUR DEBUT/CATEGORY	1994/1st

MAX GRADIENT
9%

1250m
1000
750

12.8km

0   3   6   9   12km

LES VILLARDS-S-THÔNES

ST-JEAN-DE-SIXT

D909

LA CLUSAZ

COL DE LA CROIX-FRY

D16   D909   COL DES ARAVIS

THÔNES

MANIGOD

D12

LA CLUSAZ
D909
THÔNES
TALLOIRES
D12
D909
D1212
D1508   UGINE
D216
10km

66 Col des Aravis

The Col des Aravis is a critical part of any north–south route across the Alps, forming the link between the Col du Grand Colombier and the Col des Saisies. I would have to say that the climb rising up from Flumet looks tougher on paper but in the spirit of 'La Route des Grandes Alpes', the ride described here heads south. I picked it up in Saint-Jean-de-Sixt, joining the busy D909 from the true base in Thônes and, to begin with, the slope is a very a gentle 2 to 3%. Once you reach La Clusaz, though, things start to heat up. It's a busy, convoluted town so you have to keep your eyes peeled in order to follow the signs that lead you through the steep and narrow streets. Exit, and the slope hovers around the 6% mark up to Les Etages where you head left as the road splits. From here you pass through the village into open land. Up until this point, it has not been the prettiest climb, but now it makes amends as you head up through six hairpin bends, framed by towering rock faces. Continuing at 6%, the slope allows you to ride at a healthy pace and the summit is constantly in view, then there is a brief patch of steeper road before you level, cross the brow, and roll down to continue your journey south.

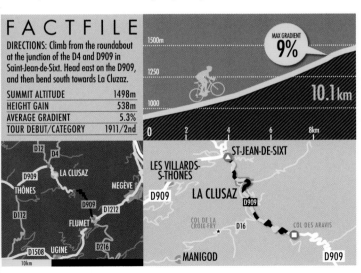

FACTFILE

DIRECTIONS: Climb from the roundabout at the junction of the D4 and D909 in Saint-Jean-de-Sixt. Head east on the D909, and then bend south towards La Cluzaz.

SUMMIT ALTITUDE	1498m
HEIGHT GAIN	538m
AVERAGE GRADIENT	5.3%
TOUR DEBUT/CATEGORY	1911/2nd

MAX GRADIENT **9%**

10.1km

1500m
1250m
1000m

0   2   4   6   8km

D12 · D4
D909 · LA CLUSAZ · MEGÈVE
THÔNES
D909 · D1212
D112
FLUMET
D1508 · UGINE · D216
10km

ST-JEAN-DE-SIXT
LES VILLARDS-S-THONES
D909 · LA CLUSAZ
D909
COL DE LA CROIX-FRY · D16 · COL DES ARAVIS
MANIGOD
D909

67 Col des Saisies

Trying to count the myriad little steep roads that rise from the valleys in the Alps would be like trying to count the stars in the Galaxy; everywhere you look there's one winding up through the trees, maybe leading to just a single house at its end. These aren't famous Cols; they're just the back roads, but ones that contain more kilometres of climbing than in the whole of my home country, England. The Col des Saisies is a more substantial road, though, and to ride from the south, start from the billiard-table-flat valley and head up the D218 from the junction with the D925. Ahead, you have 15 kilometres of varied climbing, the first half of which is reasonably tame, twisting through switchbacks, back and forth up into woods. Eight kilometres in and a short dip to the junction with the D70 bisects the climb – keep left here, following the small descent. This sharp rise will really sting your legs as your newfound momentum evaporates. The gradient is a per cent tougher for the second half, briefly touching 11%, but, on the whole, fluctuating between 6 and 9%; the scenery opens up the higher you ride, heading to the summit amidst the sprawling town of Les Saisies.

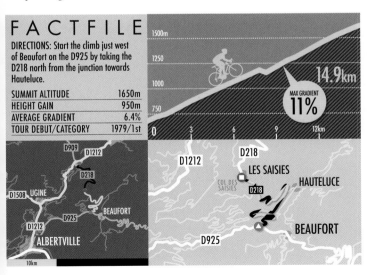

FACTFILE

DIRECTIONS: Start the climb just west of Beaufort on the D925 by taking the D218 north from the junction towards Hauteluce.

SUMMIT ALTITUDE	1650m
HEIGHT GAIN	950m
AVERAGE GRADIENT	6.4%
TOUR DEBUT/CATEGORY	1979/1st

MAX GRADIENT
11%

14.9km

68 Cormet-de-Roseland

Once at the summit, I turned to myself and said, 'At this point in time, THAT is the single greatest road you have ever ridden.' Heading north from Bourg-Saint-Maurice, the 19 kilometres that lie ahead are simply awesome – packed to the hilt with hairpins and breathtaking scenery. You begin on a 7% gradient, and then, just 2 kilometres in, the road dips. It's too soon for a rest, but you'll take it regardless, as, shortly after, the climb rears up for five solid kilometres on a 7% slope, increasing to 9%. After an arrow-straight stretch you arrive at one of the most amazing sets of bends you'll ever ride – back and forth, hairpin after hairpin, nine of them in all, squeezed into just 2 kilometres of climbing. I didn't want them to end but end they do, as, with 9 kilometres to go, you cross a narrow bridge to begin a couple of easy kilometres, which lead you into one of the greatest arenas in the Alps. From here on in it's climbing heaven as the road snakes through this giant natural amphitheatre beneath the towering rock faces and snow-covered peaks. There are bends, sheer drops, rocky outcrops, grand vistas – it has everything, and all set on a perfect 6% slope to the summit. It is just pure magic.

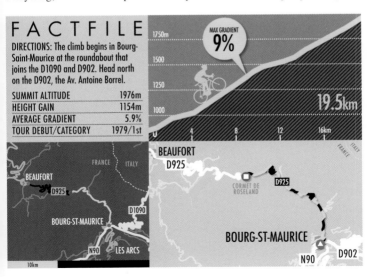

FACTFILE

DIRECTIONS: The climb begins in Bourg-Saint-Maurice at the roundabout that joins the D1090 and D902. Head north on the D902, the Av. Antoine Borrel.

SUMMIT ALTITUDE	1976m
HEIGHT GAIN	1154m
AVERAGE GRADIENT	5.9%
TOUR DEBUT/CATEGORY	1979/1st

MAX GRADIENT **9%**

19.5km

BEAUFORT D925

CORMET DE ROSELAND

D925

BOURG-ST-MAURICE

N90   D902

FRANCE   ITALY

BEAUFORT
D925

BOURG-ST-MAURICE

N90   LES ARCS

D1090

10km

69 Col du Petit-Saint-Bernard

Once you've negotiated your exit from Bourg-Saint-Maurice, the 31 kilometres of climbing that lie ahead can be split into three distinct sectors. Firstly, the shortest compromises a set of geometrically perfect zigzags that lead you up a steady 6% gradient to Villard Dessus. The second then heads into the forest and up to the first of 13 hairpins, which, to begin with, arrive with such metronomic certainty that you could set your watch by them. Straight follows bend, follows straight, all set on a perfect and very flattering 5% slope. You'll feel like a pro as you flow through the kilometres, round and up through the trees to head into the final sector that begins in La Rosière. The slope is the same blissful 5%, but the next 7 kilometres of climbing are laid out in front of you, exposed and wild. On the horizon there's a collection of turrets atop what looks like a castle. In fact, the whole environment has a fantasy feel to it, and if a unicorn had crossed my path I wouldn't have blinked. Almost at the top now, and the road ties itself in a knot before heading into the final kilometer where you pass the giant hospice to reach the border with Italy and the end of the Col du Petit Saint Bernard. A climb with lots of bark, but not so much bite.

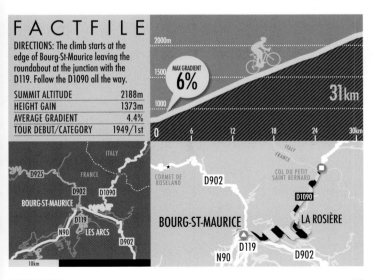

FACTFILE

DIRECTIONS: The climb starts at the edge of Bourg-St-Maurice leaving the roundabout at the junction with the D119. Follow the D1090 all the way.

SUMMIT ALTITUDE	2188m
HEIGHT GAIN	1373m
AVERAGE GRADIENT	4.4%
TOUR DEBUT/CATEGORY	1949/1st

MAX GRADIENT
6%

31km

70 Col de Tamié

Climbing out of Albertville, the host town of the 1992 Winter Olympics, there are many ways to reach the summit of the Col de Tamié – from the north, south-east, and west. This straightforward route avoids the town centre and follows the D990 heading south-west to the base. Turning abruptly right, opposite a pharmacy, I began to climb on the Route de Tamié, dead straight to begin with, and then banking left as the road begins to snake to and fro towards Gémilly. Still in the outskirts of Albertville, the slopes are pretty much 7% all the way, with the odd stretch to test the legs but nothing that will unsettle you. With 7 kilometres to go, you reach the first of two junctions: head straight on to make your way to the second one at 4 kilometres to go, where you leave the D64 and join the D201C. It's a mixture of neat open fields and patchy woodland for the rest of the journey and although ever so slightly tougher, there's nothing to stop you really enjoying this climb. Packed with switchbacks, some of which will force you from the saddle, these last 4 kilometres offer up fantastic views all the way to the top and the junction with the D104.

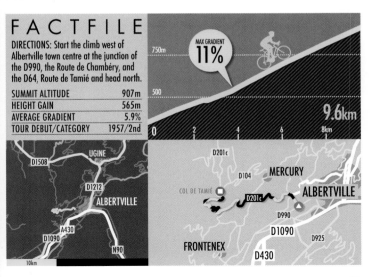

FACTFILE

DIRECTIONS: Start the climb west of Albertville town centre at the junction of the D990, the Route de Chambéry, and the D64, Route de Tamié and head north.

SUMMIT ALTITUDE	907m
HEIGHT GAIN	565m
AVERAGE GRADIENT	5.9%
TOUR DEBUT/CATEGORY	1957/2nd

MAX GRADIENT **11%**

750m
500

9.6km

0   2   4   6   8km

D1508   UGINE
D1212
ALBERTVILLE
A430
D1090
N90
10km

D201c
D104   MERCURY
COL DE TAMIÉ   D201c   ALBERTVILLE
D990
D1090   D925
FRONTENEX
D430

71 Col du Grand Cucheron

Crossing the ridge linking the D1006 to the D925, the Col du Grand Cucheron has had a part to play in the Tour since 1972 when the great Eddy Merckx was the first to cross its summit. To begin with, the road rises straight up through Saint-Pierre-de-Belleville, not too tough, just creeping above 6%. A few kilometres in, you reach the junction with the D73: head sharp left. It's steep through a couple of switchbacks, and then the gradient vanishes before you continue to the mother of all false flats. Immediately, you change into a larger gear but undetectable to the naked eye the slope is ever so gently becoming steeper. Now the mind is still saying it's flat, and it certainly looks flat, but the legs – well, they're starting to disagree. The actual effort needed to climb is now much greater than the perceived effort to climb. You want to click down a gear, but that would mean giving in to the road, so you just push on. This torment ends where the road banks right to start switching back and forth on a proper slope, which touches 13% in places! The last 4 kilometres are consistently hard, with the distance between each bend decreasing after every turn until you round a 90-degree left-hand bend to finish, enveloped by the silent forest.

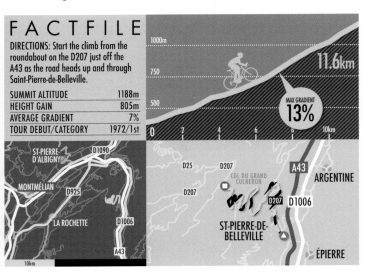

FACTFILE

DIRECTIONS: Start the climb from the roundabout on the D207 just off the A43 as the road heads up and through Saint-Pierre-de-Belleville.

SUMMIT ALTITUDE	1188m
HEIGHT GAIN	805m
AVERAGE GRADIENT	7%
TOUR DEBUT/CATEGORY	1972/1st

11.6km

MAX GRADIENT 13%

ST-PIERRE D'ALBIGNY — D1090
MONTMÉLIAN — D925
LA ROCHETTE — D1006
A43
10km

D25 — D207
D207
COL DU GRAND CUCHERON
D207 — D1006
A43 — ARGENTINE
ST-PIERRE-DE-BELLEVILLE
ÉPIERRE

72 Col du Granier

I planned to start this climb on the D912, but due to road works I was forced to find an alternative route. It proved to be a blessing in disguise, as it led me to the brilliant Boulevard de Bellevue. Heading due south you're thrust straight into a collection of five hairpins that rise sharply out of Chambéry to the mini-roundabout where you join up with the D912. A kilometre further on, passing through Bellecombette, the road briefly dips, turns sharp right, and then, with 11 kilometres to go, heads into the hardest part of the climb. At only 8% it's no leg breaker, but it will have you clicking down a few sprockets and breathing a little harder. You'll now see looming above you a giant rock face, standing like an impenetrable fortress in front of a solitary warrior. Somehow you must thwart its defences: bank hard right, scouting along the road that hugs the jagged stone wall. Looking for a weakness, a way over, suddenly an opening appears: a tunnel, and your gateway through to the Chartreuse. All that's left now is the push to the summit. Starting on a 4% slope and ramping up to touch under 7%, it's never a chore to ride, although the last kilometre does drag a little up to the summit at the small café.

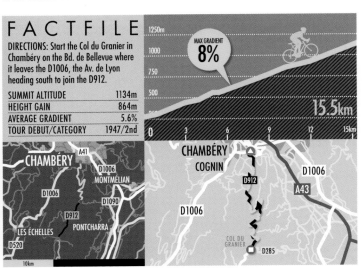

FACTFILE

DIRECTIONS: Start the Col du Granier in Chambéry on the Bd. de Bellevue where it leaves the D1006, the Av. de Lyon heading south to join the D912.

SUMMIT ALTITUDE	1134m
HEIGHT GAIN	864m
AVERAGE GRADIENT	5.6%
TOUR DEBUT/CATEGORY	1947/2nd

MAX GRADIENT
8%

15.5km

CHAMBÉRY
A41
D1006
MONTMÉLIAN
D1006
D1090
D912
PONTCHARRA
LES ÉCHELLES
D520
10km

CHAMBÉRY
COGNIN
D912
D1006
A43
D1006
COL DU GRANIER
D285

73 Col du Cucheron

The Col du Cucheron is the second of the three climbs that traverse the Massif de la Chartreuse, linking Chambéry to the north with Grenoble in the south. Leaving the sleepy town of Saint-Pierre-d'Entremont and the surroundings of its exquisite valley, you follow the signs out to Grenoble. Once free of the town you immediately double back on yourself up a sharp, but thankfully short, 20% hairpin before settling down to climb a 7% slope for close to 4 kilometres. Squiggling a little, but heading predominantly south, the road very briefly levels into Chenevey before climbing out the other side into dense forest. Up next is a short descent into Saint Philibert, so gather some speed as you'll want to carry as much momentum into the final 2 kilometres as you can. Up ahead you'll see the base of a giant 'V' on the horizon and that's your goal – that's the summit. Up through the forest, the road sweeping right and then left delivers you to the start of a very hard last kilometre. Set on a 9% slope, and feeling much harder in places, you're really made to work for this one; round each bend, you hope it's the last, but they keep on coming, until finally, the brow appears – you cross it and head on to the Col de Porte.

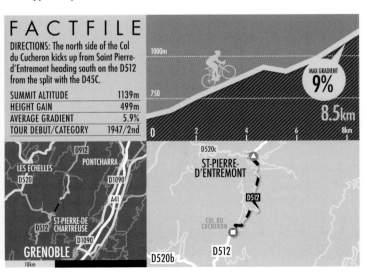

FACTFILE

DIRECTIONS: The north side of the Col du Cucheron kicks up from Saint Pierre-d'Entremont heading south on the D512 from the split with the D45C.

SUMMIT ALTITUDE	1139m
HEIGHT GAIN	499m
AVERAGE GRADIENT	5.9%
TOUR DEBUT/CATEGORY	1947/2nd

MAX GRADIENT **9%**

8.5km

D520c

ST-PIERRE-D'ENTREMONT

D512

COL DU CUCHERON

D512

D520b

D912

PONTCHARRA

LES ECHELLES

D520

D1090

A41

ST-PIERRE-DE CHARTREUSE

D512

D1090

GRENOBLE

10km

74 Col de Porte

Call me a wimp, but I rode the easy side of the Col de Porte, which at only 8.3 kilometres is less than half the length of the southern side rising out of Grenoble. This again opened the debate as to whether I'd picked the best side to write about because, as always, there was time to ride only the one – so which would it be? Well, a choice had to be made, and this time the fact that I was heading south and had ridden the two previous climbs heading south all but decided it, but of course all other factors had to be taken into consideration. So, to ride the northern face, start the climb in La Diat in front of a giant abandoned hotel, cross a small bridge and head upwards. The opening salvos feel quite tough even though the slope is only 6% rising to 7%, and then, with 4 kilometres to go, you enter thick forest and it's time to leave the comfort zone as the slope ramps up to 9%. The thick canopy overhead breaks here and there, illuminating your progress as you creep into the last kilometre, where the gradient falls back to 7%. Up ahead there's a sign for the summit, you pick up some speed, but alas you're not there yet – you still have to round one final corner before you reach the finish at the brow.

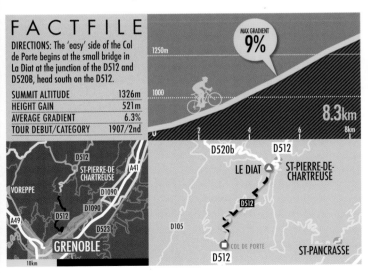

FACTFILE

DIRECTIONS: The 'easy' side of the Col de Porte begins at the small bridge in La Diat at the junction of the D512 and D520B, head south on the D512.

SUMMIT ALTITUDE	1326m
HEIGHT GAIN	521m
AVERAGE GRADIENT	6.3%
TOUR DEBUT/CATEGORY	1907/2nd

MAX GRADIENT
9%

1250m

1000

8.3km

8km

D520b · D512

LE DIAT · ST-PIERRE-DE-CHARTREUSE

ST-PIERRE-DE-CHARTREUSE · A41

VOREPPE · D1090

D1090

D512 · D523

A49

GRENOBLE

10km

D105

D512

COL DE PORTE

D512

ST-PANCRASSE

75 Col de la Madeleine

If you're heading to the Tour, and if the route is using the Col de la Madeleine, then there is no better mountain on which to base yourself for unrestricted views of the racing. The final 3 kilometres provide an almost-perfect viewing gallery, with a multitude of vantage points, all with a clear line of sight to track the peloton's progress as it inches upwards. Of course you have to get there first, so head out of La Chambre, pass the 19-kilometres-to-go sign – and it's hard, hard from the start. The slope – between 8.5 and 9% and steeper still through the corners – writhes and contorts its way upwards through a collection of villages. Whenever you feel comfortable, it breaks your rhythm, whenever you feel the slope ease, it bites back, and it's not until 11 kilometres to go that it offers any respite. If you glance up here you'll catch sight of the summit high above you, but there is still a long haul. Through Longchamp, you leave all signs of habitation behind and enter the giant switchbacks that cut left and right across a beautiful Alpine meadow. Clear of the treeline, stacking one on top of another, these challenging final slopes deliver you to the peak of one of cycling's greatest arenas.

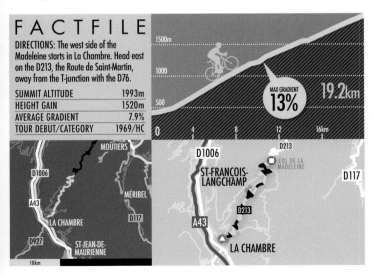

FACTFILE

DIRECTIONS: The west side of the Madeleine starts in La Chambre. Head east on the D213, the Route de Saint-Martin, away from the T-junction with the D76.

SUMMIT ALTITUDE	1993m
HEIGHT GAIN	1520m
AVERAGE GRADIENT	7.9%
TOUR DEBUT/CATEGORY	1969/HC

MAX GRADIENT **13%**   **19.2km**

MOÛTIERS

D1006

MÉRIBEL

A43

LA CHAMBRE   D117

D927   ST-JEAN-DE-MAURIENNE

10km

D1006   D213

COL DE LA MADELEINE

ST-FRANCOIS-LANGCHAMP   D117

D213

A43

LA CHAMBRE

76 Courchevel

The first time I rode up to Courchevel was on a visit to the 2005 Tour, as it was the first mountaintop finish of that year's race. Positioned in a prime spot, we sat waiting all day to see who would round the bend first and therefore claim the mantle of race favourite. Hoping, praying, that finally, after six years of domination, it would be someone other than Lance Armstrong, our hopes were shattered as guess who appeared first? And the rest, as they say, was all lies. Courchevel is a very busy climb, with the ride from Moûtiers to the base verging on dangerous at times, but once you're heading up through the bends things calm down. Still, it's no remote pass – chalets, shops, and hotels line almost all the 7 to 10% slopes. There are interludes of beauty, particularly with 6 kilometres to go, but you're soon plunged back into another village or town, and then, as you enter Courcheval 1850, the route to the summit becomes very convoluted. I found the key was to look for the signs to the heliport – there are plenty of them – and if you keep your eyes peeled they'll lead you through it all to ride at last over some exposed land to the dead end at the top.

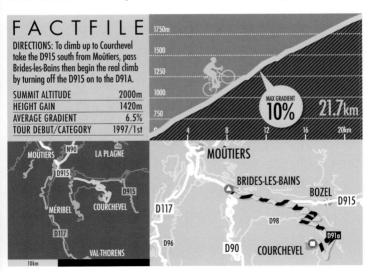

FACTFILE

DIRECTIONS: To climb up to Courchevel take the D915 south from Moûtiers, pass Brides-les-Bains then begin the real climb by turning off the D915 on to the D91A.

SUMMIT ALTITUDE	2000m
HEIGHT GAIN	1420m
AVERAGE GRADIENT	6.5%
TOUR DEBUT/CATEGORY	1997/1st

MAX GRADIENT 10%   21.7km

77 La Plagne

A climb in the Alps, up to a ski resort, with twenty-one hairpin bends – that's Alpe d'Huez, right? Well, not this time. This is the climb up to La Plagne. Yes, it has twenty-one hairpin bends but that's where the similarities end, because this road is longer, harder, and – best of all – it's much quieter. Start the climb by dropping out of Aime, under the N90, and then up through Mâcot to the small roundabout where you head right. In homage to the great Alpe, each of its bends is marked with a sign to count you through them. None are named after champions who've won at the top, though; they have more cryptic names like 'cote rouge', which in my state of partial exhaustion I translate as 'Code Red'! Starting at around 8%, the gradient takes a turn for the worse as you reach 13 kilometres to go and ramps up to 10% with the bends now coming thick and fast. Flirting between 8, 9, and 10%, it's not until the impressive sight of the 1992 Olympic bobsleigh run comes into to view, with 5 kilometres to go, that things ease up. Set on a 5% slope, the final 2 kilometres wind through the town to finish at the base of myriad ski runs on top of the best twenty-one-bend climb in the Alps – just don't tell anyone in Alpe d'Huez I said that.

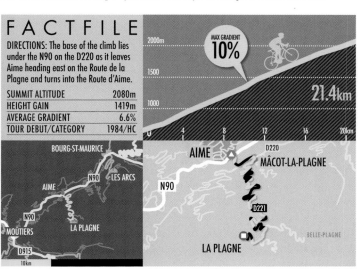

FACTFILE

DIRECTIONS: The base of the climb lies under the N90 on the D220 as it leaves Aime heading east on the Route de la Plagne and turns into the Route d'Aime.

SUMMIT ALTITUDE	2080m
HEIGHT GAIN	1419m
AVERAGE GRADIENT	6.6%
TOUR DEBUT/CATEGORY	1984/HC

MAX GRADIENT
10%

2000m
1500
1000

21.4km

0   4   8   12   16   20km

BOURG-ST-MAURICE

AIME   △   D220

MÂCOT-LA-PLAGNE

N90   LES ARCS

AIME

N90

D221

N90

MOÛTIERS

LA PLAGNE

BELLE-PLAGNE

D915

LA PLAGNE

10km

78 Col de l'Iseran

The Col de l'Iseran is utterly breathtaking, and to quote one of my old mentors, Chris Sidwells, 'It feels more Himalayan at the top than Alpine.' I rode from the south and started my ascent in the small town of Bonneval-sur-Arc, which lies hunkered down in the safety of the serene valley. Up steep right away and dead straight for a kilometre you then bend back on yourself for much more of the same until, with 9 kilometres to go, you're gifted a kilometre of flat. I'd make the most of it because what lies ahead is just nasty. Over the next 6 kilometres, again and again it ramps up over 10%. It is just brutal on the legs, and it's exposed – there's not an inch of shelter or shade the whole way. At 3 kilometres to go there is one final respite where the road crosses a small bridge before you start, I swear, some of the hardest climbing in this book. Maybe it was the 35°C heat down in the valley, or the cumulative effort to reach this point, but these last 3 kilometres had me on the ropes. Pedal rev after pedal rev, up, past vast swathes of ice and snow I toiled in the noticeably thin air, round one final corner, finishing at 2,770m beneath the clattering of flags on the beautifully exposed, wind ravaged summit. SIMPLY AWESOME.

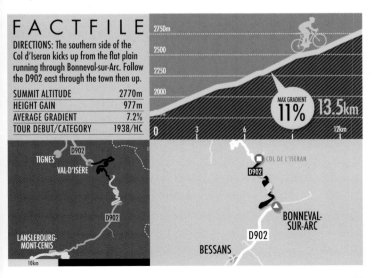

FACTFILE

DIRECTIONS: The southern side of the Col d'Iseran kicks up from the flat plain running through Bonneval-sur-Arc. Follow the D902 east through the town then up.

SUMMIT ALTITUDE	2770m
HEIGHT GAIN	977m
AVERAGE GRADIENT	7.2%
TOUR DEBUT/CATEGORY	1938/HC

MAX GRADIENT **11%** 13.5km

TIGNES
D902
VAL-D'ISÈRE
D902
LANSLEBOURG-MONT-CENIS
10km

COL DE L'ISERAN
D902
BONNEVAL-SUR-ARC
D902
BESSANS

79 Col du Mont-Cenis

Looking at the Col du Mont-Cenis on the map, it is the very picture of the ideal mountain road with its five hairpin bends equally distributed along the route from base to summit. You start climbing in Lanslebourg-Mont-Cenis where the D1006, which enters town from the west, turns south, heading for Italy. The gradient is a steady 5% on the opening kilometres and the legs feel good, but the legs always feel good at the bottom of a mountain – it's at the top that they hurt. Once round the first hairpin, the climbing becomes a bit more of a challenge, ramping up to 8% and remaining like this almost to the peak. Eight per cent marks the edge of my comfort zone. I can ride all day on 7% and most of the day on 8%, but when it climbs over 8% then I really start to feel it. I pretty much discovered my 'gradient threshold' on the first mountain I rode and I'm sure you'll find yours in the same way. Anyway, back to the climb. Head through the remaining four hairpins trying to keep your tempo even, and then leaving them behind head up on to the plateau for the push to the summit. In the shadow of mountains, the last kilometre eases back to a nice 6%, which allows you to click through the gears and finish with a sprint!

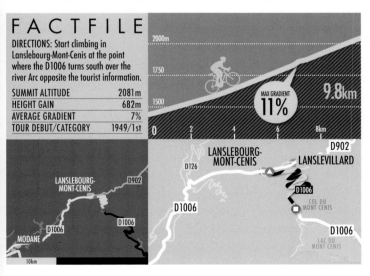

FACTFILE

DIRECTIONS: Start climbing in Lanslebourg-Mont-Cenis at the point where the D1006 turns south over the river Arc opposite the tourist information.

SUMMIT ALTITUDE	2081m
HEIGHT GAIN	682m
AVERAGE GRADIENT	7%
TOUR DEBUT/CATEGORY	1949/1st

MAX GRADIENT 11%

9.8km

2000m
1750
1500

0   2   4   6   8km

LANSLEBOURG-MONT-CENIS
D126
D902
LANSLEVILLARD
D1006
COL DU MONT CENIS
D1006
LAC DU MONT CENIS

LANSLEBOURG-MONT-CENIS
D902
D1006
D1006
MODANE
10km

80 La Toussuire

The climb up to La Toussuire begins in Saint-Jean-de-Maurienne, the birthplace of the Opinel pocket knife, so it's fitting that there's a giant sculpture of the famous blade set in the centre of the roundabout at its base. Heading south-east, the wide, busy and soon-to-be dead-straight road is a real slog; it is crushingly heavy on the legs as you crawl upwards past the imposing quarry on your right. I hate steep, straight, and wide roads like this, and thankfully the purgatory ends where it splits; you keep right, the scenery improves, and the gradient eases back. The transformation to beautiful mountain road is instant as you begin to twist skyward though sleepy villages ringed by stunning views. Up ahead, the road splits again. I'd originally planned to ride left through La Corbier, but an error led me right and this proved to be by far the better route. The Tour heads left through the ski resort for obvious commercial reasons but it's an ugly and cluttered road when compared with the much quieter meander through neat grassland. Both paths have short bursts of steep 8% gradient, and both deliver you to the same finale, a short ramp at the apex of the loop into the centre of La Toussuire.

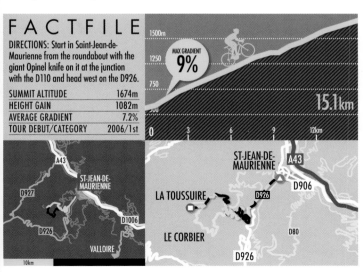

FACTFILE

DIRECTIONS: Start in Saint-Jean-de-Maurienne from the roundabout with the giant Opinel knife on it at the junction with the D110 and head west on the D926.

SUMMIT ALTITUDE	1674m
HEIGHT GAIN	1082m
AVERAGE GRADIENT	7.2%
TOUR DEBUT/CATEGORY	2006/1st

MAX GRADIENT
9%

15.1km

81 Col du Glandon

I'd previously descended this side of the Glandon three times and hated every minute of it. Its relentless corners in and out of woodland really wear you down, so I'd hoped to enjoy climbing it more, but, oh, was I in for a shock. It is a massive 20 kilometres to the top and starts on gentle slopes, climbing below 7% for the first 4 kilometres before it stiffens to 8%. At halfway, there's a refreshing 1,500m of almost flat riding and the dilemma is, as always, 'to big ring or not to big ring'. Then into the second half and it gets steeper with stretches of 9% awaiting your legs. I'd started the climb in light drizzle, but soon the ability to observe my surroundings was severely hindered as I rode right into an electrical storm. Flashes of lightening illuminated the mass of cloud that enveloped me, thunder bounced off the mountainsides, and the rain fell harder and harder. I wasn't sure of the statistics for cyclists killed each year by lightning, but I didn't want to become one of them; equally, I wanted to reach the top. I entered the final 2 kilometres, both set on a 10% gradient but with just 700m to go I threw in the towel. I turned and fled, starting by far the most unpleasant descent of any mountain I've ever ridden.

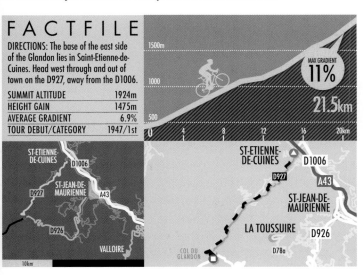

FACTFILE

DIRECTIONS: The base of the east side of the Glandon lies in Saint-Etienne-de-Cuines. Head west through and out of town on the D927, away from the D1006.

SUMMIT ALTITUDE	1924m
HEIGHT GAIN	1475m
AVERAGE GRADIENT	6.9%
TOUR DEBUT/CATEGORY	1947/1st

MAX GRADIENT **11%**

21.5km

ST-ETIENNE-DE-CUINES · D1006
D927 · ST-JEAN-DE-MAURIENNE · A43
D926 · VALLOIRE
10km

ST-ETIENNE-DE-CUINES · D1006 · A43
D927 · ST-JEAN-DE-MAURIENNE
LA TOUSSUIRE · D926
COL DU GLANDON · D78a

82 Col de la Croix de Fer

The Croix de Fer is a monster of a climb and there are three distinct ways to the top: South out of Saint-Étienne-de-Cuines, north from Rochetaillée, and again south from Saint-Jean-de-Maurienne – although I wouldn't wish this last route on even my worst enemy, it is simply hideous. I've picked the route north. You start this by zigzagging up the side of the dam at the head of Lac du Verney. It's easy-going for a while, then you rise into the forest where it is often as steep as 10% but also rewards you with the first of two significant drops. Clusters of hairpins break the climb's steady upward progression, the last of which are the most dramatic as they drag you from the trees and deliver you to the head of the stunning Lac de Grand Maison. For a while, it's hard to ride a straight line as you soak up the beauty of this lake set beneath the surrounding snow-capped peaks, but track along its edge and you'll reach the second drop. Crossing the exposed tundra up to the turn for the summit of the Col de Glandon and then following the road right, you will see the iron cross that marks the finish. It's a grind to reach, but once over the brow, you're rewarded with the most breathtaking, stunningly beautiful view in the whole of the Alps.

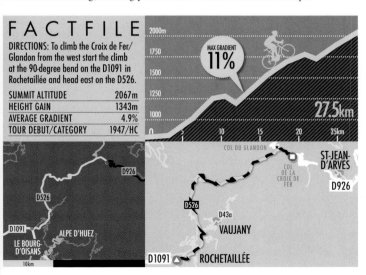

FACTFILE

DIRECTIONS: To climb the Croix de Fer/Glandon from the west start the climb at the 90-degree bend on the D1091 in Rochetaillée and head east on the D526.

SUMMIT ALTITUDE	2067m
HEIGHT GAIN	1343m
AVERAGE GRADIENT	4.9%
TOUR DEBUT/CATEGORY	1947/HC

MAX GRADIENT
11%

2000m
1750
1500
1250
1000

27.5km

0   5   10   15   20   25km

COL DU GLANDON

ST-JEAN-D'ARVES

COL DE LA CROIX DE FER

D926

D926

D526

D43a

VAUJANY

D1091   ROCHETAILLÉE

D1091

LE BOURG-D'OISANS

ALPE D'HUEZ

D526

10km

83 Alpe d'Huez

It's not the longest, not the steepest, and certainly not the hardest, but Alpe d'Huez is THE mountain all cyclists want to climb. There's more cycling history etched into its twenty-one famous bends than some entire countries can boast, so day or night, rain or shine, there are always riders leaving their mark on its slopes. As you exit Bourg-d'Oisans, the transition from calm, pan-flat valley to vicious climbing is immediate and will rip your legs to shreds, and what's more, you'll not have a chance to catch your breath for four solid, back-breaking kilometres. By the time this opening onslaught is over, you will have spent an age in the red and the legs will be begging for mercy. Thankfully their cries are heard and the slope eases – not completely, but enough for you to find a comfortable rhythm through the hairpins. Each bend, marked with a plaque naming a rider who has won a stage at the top, becomes more than just a history lesson: it acts as a carrot to aim for, a goal to reach as you push yourself to record your best time. Leaving the final hairpin, the subsequent ramp will leave you empty, but you must drive on through the final kilometre, following the signs through town, to cross the official finishing line.

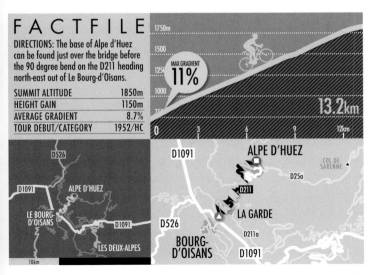

FACTFILE

DIRECTIONS: The base of Alpe d'Huez can be found just over the bridge before the 90 degree bend on the D211 heading north-east out of Le Bourg-d'Oisans.

SUMMIT ALTITUDE	1850m
HEIGHT GAIN	1150m
AVERAGE GRADIENT	8.7%
TOUR DEBUT/CATEGORY	1952/HC

MAX GRADIENT **11%**

13.2km

84 Col d'Ornon

In each of the four years I rode The Marmotte (see page 12), this was my acclimatization climb, my road of choice to prime the body for the challenge ahead. After the long drive south to the Alps, it is essential to give your legs a spin the day before, and this climb is the perfect way to loosen them up without stressing them too much before the big day. It's not just the gradient but the Col d'Ornon's location that makes it the perfect warm-up climb as it lies just a couple of minutes north of Le Bourg-d'Oisans. At 10 kilometres it is no walk in the park, but it's never steep for long and has plenty of significant patches of respite. You begin the climb heading west on the D526 riding in the shadow of jagged rock faces, their surfaces disintegrating behind the trappings of wire mesh. Over to your left there is a drop-off so severe that you're riding eye to eye with the tops of the giant pines that stand in the bottom of the valley, with just a 1m wall protecting you from oblivion. The middle of the climb is marked by a dip, then a level, and with your legs well and truly awake, gently spin them for the remaining 5 kilometres to the top through the sedate farmland and scattered houses – then

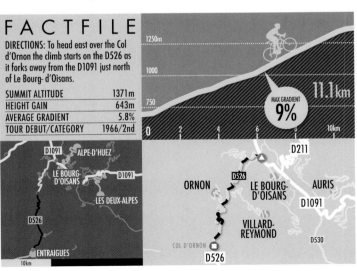

FACTFILE

DIRECTIONS: To head east over the Col d'Ornon the climb starts on the D526 as it forks away from the D1091 just north of Le Bourg- d'Oisans.

SUMMIT ALTITUDE	1371m
HEIGHT GAIN	643m
AVERAGE GRADIENT	5.8%
TOUR DEBUT/CATEGORY	1966/2nd

MAX GRADIENT **9%**

11.1km

85 Les Deux Alpes

It can't be easy to live your life in the shadow of Alpe d'Huez, always the bridesmaid and never the bride, but that's Les Deuz Alpes' lot in life. It will never match the fame of its flamboyant counterpart, but judged on its own merits it's a great climb with a much more attractive summit than its big brother across the valley. Starting abruptly as the D213 kicks up away from the Lac du Chambon, the gradient is a uniform and testing 8%, and, in an attempt to mimic the great alp next door, Les Deux Alpes has taken the bold move to number each of its hairpins. Instead of the infamous twenty-one bends, it only boasts ten, but that's still more than many can muster. Through the first four and with 6 kilometres to the summit, you reach the roundabout at Mont-de-Lans where you head straight across, up a little further, and then drop down under a bridge. Stick it in the big ring and take that momentum into the rest of the climb, which alternates between 7, 8, and 9%. It's hard going up through the remaining bends, the last four of which are a tightly packed set of perfect alpine zigzags. Leaving the final bend, you line up for the summit; it's a bit of a drag, but the reward at the finish is one of the most attractive ski villages in the Alps.

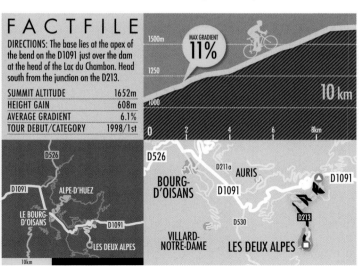

FACTFILE

DIRECTIONS: The base lies at the apex of the bend on the D1091 just over the dam at the head of the Lac du Chambon. Head south from the junction on the D213.

SUMMIT ALTITUDE	1652m
HEIGHT GAIN	608m
AVERAGE GRADIENT	6.1%
TOUR DEBUT/CATEGORY	1998/1st

MAX GRADIENT
11%

1500m
1250
1000
0   2   4   6   8km

10 km

D526
D1091
ALPE-D'HUEZ
LE BOURG-
D'OISANS
D1091
LES DEUX ALPES
10km

D526
D211a AURIS
BOURG-
D'OISANS D1091
D1091
D530
VILLARD-
NOTRE-DAME
D213
LES DEUX ALPES

86 Col du Télégraphe

This is the very first mountain I ever rode, where I broke my duck on an eventful trip chasing after the 1992 Tour. We parked our bus at the bottom, hopped out, and went straight up, and a more perfect introduction to the sublime act of cycling up a mountain I could not have wished for. The ability to climb for close to an hour, non-stop, was just totally alien, and the gain in altitude, the views – that was the kind of experience I had imagined could be achieved only by flying, and I'd done it under my own steam. The Telegraph is a perfect 12 kilometres of seemingly endless swirling bends set on a gradient that hovers between 5% and just shy of 10%, the only real stain being the run-down industry in the valley at the base. You're soon away from Saint-Michel-de-Maurienne and climbing through the smaller villages that punctuate the lower slopes, bend after bend through the thick forest. It's not until you're closing in on the summit that the forest starts to thin and you're allowed more prolonged eyefuls of the majestic view. On my first ascent I must have stopped ten times to take pictures before reaching the summit and beginning the short descent into Valloire at the base of the climb of the mighty Galibier.

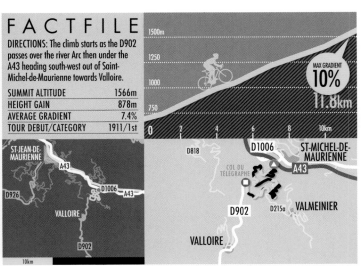

FACTFILE

DIRECTIONS: The climb starts as the D902 passes over the river Arc then under the A43 heading south-west out of Saint-Michel-de-Maurienne towards Valloire.

SUMMIT ALTITUDE	1566m
HEIGHT GAIN	878m
AVERAGE GRADIENT	7.4%
TOUR DEBUT/CATEGORY	1911/1st

MAX GRADIENT
10%
11.8km

87 Col du Galibier

I've had the best of legs and I've had the worst of legs on this mountain; I've soared like an eagle and died like a dog. It can be both utterly unforgiving and unbelievably rewarding all at once. Leaving the hub of Valloire, you begin the first half of the climb – wearing but never challenging – tracking up the valley for 2 kilometres in the shadow of mind-blowing, scree-covered slopes. Up next is arguably the most vividly defined halfway point of any climb: double back on yourself, round to the right and the road turns up to eleven! At first dead straight, the viciously steep incline then contorts upon itself, pulling you out of the valley to deliver you into a hostile, boulder-strewn environment. Once the road begins to straighten, you've 6 kilometres of brutal climbing ahead. Free from one set of bends you cross the plateau before entering an even more convoluted set. From above, the road resembles a go-kart track as it ties itself in a series of knots which lead you to the final kilometre – and what a final kilometre! It lasts an eternity, every metre set on a punishing 10% slope; you grind your way to the summit, which will be lined with thick snow and ice even at the height of summer.

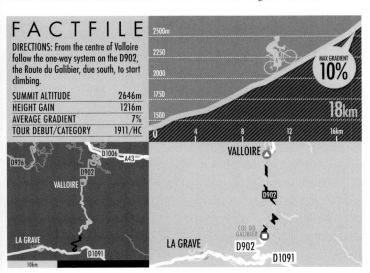

FACTFILE

DIRECTIONS: From the centre of Valloire follow the one-way system on the D902, the Route du Galibier, due south, to start climbing.

SUMMIT ALTITUDE	2646m
HEIGHT GAIN	1216m
AVERAGE GRADIENT	7%
TOUR DEBUT/CATEGORY	1911/HC

MAX GRADIENT 10%

18km

VALLOIRE

D902

COL DU GALIBIER

LA GRAVE   D902

D1091

ALPES
DU SUD

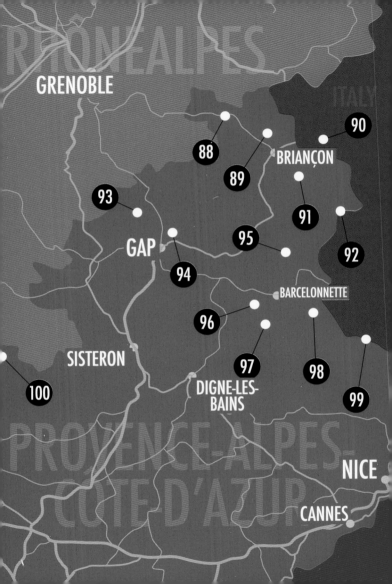

88 Col du Lautaret

A stalwart of the Tour and a vital link between the north and south Alps, the Col du Lautaret has been used in pretty much every edition for the past 60 years. A convoluted and complicated route from the north, the climb from the south described here is much more straightforward. Leaving Briançon the road rises on a gentle 3% slope to Saint-Chaffrey before passing through village after village, rising and falling for 8 kilometres, and then settling into constant climbing. Still very gentle, the road makes its way to Le Monêtier-les-Bains and the scenery opens up as you make your way through the beautiful valley, framed by snow-capped peaks. For close to 7 kilometres, the road lines out in front of you, now set on a slightly tougher but still relatively tame 5% gradient. Passing a few abandoned tunnel entrances, you round a small headland – the only significant deviation in the path from Briançon – and pass through a shelter/tunnel to enter the final twisting kilometre. As the slope eases you arrive at the summit, surrounded by a collection of restaurants, in the shadow of the giant Lautaret glacier at the base of the 'easy' side of the Col du Galibier.

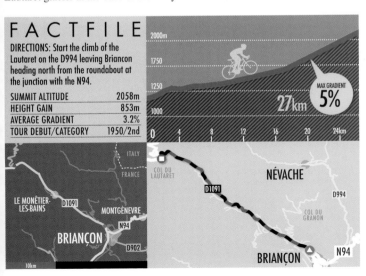

FACTFILE

DIRECTIONS: Start the climb of the Lautaret on the D994 leaving Briancon heading north from the roundabout at the junction with the N94.

SUMMIT ALTITUDE	2058m
HEIGHT GAIN	853m
AVERAGE GRADIENT	3.2%
TOUR DEBUT/CATEGORY	1950/2nd

27km   MAX GRADIENT 5%

2000m · 1750 · 1250 · 1000 · 0 · 4 · 8 · 12 · 16 · 20 · 24km

ITALY
FRANCE
COL DU LAUTARET
LE MONÊTIER-LES-BAINS   D1091
D1091
MONTGENEVRE
N94
NÉVACHE
D994
COL DU GRANON
BRIANÇON
D902
10km
BRIANÇON   N94

89 Col du Granon

I can count on one hand how many times I wished I'd fitted a compact chain set whilst researching this book and three of them were on this climb. It's not all that famous, and to date the Tour has used the climb only once, but my god it's tough. Leaving Saint-Chaffrey, the sign says 11.4 kilometres to the top and right away it's steep, as the narrow, rugged road weaves its way out of the valley. With 8 kilometres to go, the slope averages 9% – steeper in places but thankfully easier in others – as it makes its way to open ground. When you pass the 6-kilometre-to-go mark, though, all hell breaks loose; I swear, I hardly touched with my saddle from here to the summit, for six whole kilometres. First 9%, then 10%, then 11%, then back to 9% and once more rising up over 10%. There's no rest, no break – just endless, unrelenting punishment across a harsh, featureless but beautiful mountainside. Burned by the sun, eaten alive by horseflies, blinded by suncream and sweat running into my eyes, I toiled up this savage climb inch by inch. Eventually you reach the last kilometre, but it is one that lasts an eternity, you'll be searching round each bend, hoping it will lead to the summit, and then at last you make it, and the road – it just ends. OUCH.

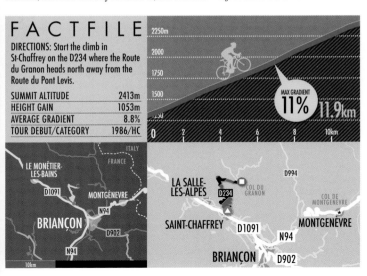

FACTFILE

DIRECTIONS: Start the climb in St-Chaffrey on the D234 where the Route du Granon heads north away from the Route du Pont Levis.

SUMMIT ALTITUDE	2413m
HEIGHT GAIN	1053m
AVERAGE GRADIENT	8.8%
TOUR DEBUT/CATEGORY	1986/HC

MAX GRADIENT 11% 11.9km

Even though the Tour has visited many countries over the years, there are only three climbs in this book outside the borders of France: the two in Andorra and this one up to the resort of Sestriere in Italy. It was on this mountain, on the 18th of July 1992, that the Italian Claudio Chiappucci rode to one of the greatest victories in Tour history. He attacked – almost from the drop of the flag – with 245 kilometres and five mountains in front of him, to win alone, here in his native Italy, to the utter delight of his adoring *tifosi*. At the time it was the greatest climbing I'd ever seen – the drama, the effort, the emotion – and I knew one day I would have to visit this climb and ride its slopes myself. To begin, leave the cobbled streets of Oulx and head south up the steady 10-kilometre drag to Cesana Torinese where the proper climbing starts. Breaking left at the roundabout, you face 3 kilometres of stiff 8% before 2.5 of relaxing flat where you can recharge your batteries before the slope ramps up to 9%. Through two tough kilometres and the rest of the climb is set on a gentle 6%, which delivers you into the centre of Sestriere, but alas, not into a crowd of 10,000 Italians all shouting your name.

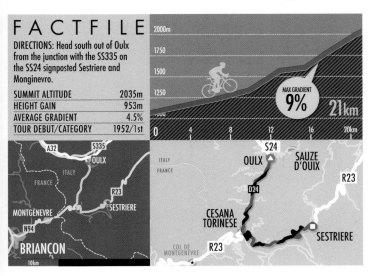

FACTFILE

DIRECTIONS: Head south out of Oulx from the junction with the SS335 on the SS24 signposted Sestriere and Monginevro.

SUMMIT ALTITUDE	2035m
HEIGHT GAIN	953m
AVERAGE GRADIENT	4.5%
TOUR DEBUT/CATEGORY	1952/1st

MAX GRADIENT
9%

21km

91 Col d'Izoard

I am not a big fan of the first 9 kilometres of this climb, but I just love the last 10. It's a bit of a faff to reach the base, but there are plenty of signs, so hopefully you won't get lost, and then when you do find the Avenue du Col-d'Izoard it's steep right away – a real shock to the system. Once through the first 2 kilometres, the road levels and then drops for a kilometre before it's up once more, this time to 7%. Your cadence falls, your speed vanishes, and you begin the trudge up though the valley to Cervières where the complexion of the road changes and you head due south into the beauty of the mountains. On a hot day, you'll be deafened by the sound of the crickets as they launch themselves from the verges into the road, pinging off your spokes to fall prone on the tough 8 to 9% slopes. Trying to avoid them, you head straight for a while, through Le Laus, then into five wonderful kilometres of twists and turns. The tangled road is littered with shallow sweeping corners and vicious 20% ramps, as it cuts its way up through the forest. Once you pass the last tree, all that's left is the ride across the awesome, scree-littered, alien landscape to finish at the large monument that marks the summit.

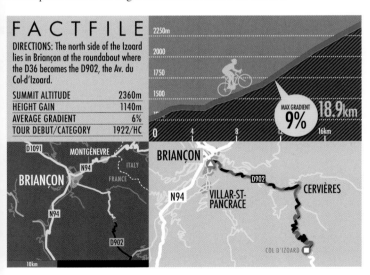

FACTFILE

DIRECTIONS: The north side of the Izoard lies in Briançon at the roundabout where the D36 becomes the D902, the Av. du Col-d'Izoard.

SUMMIT ALTITUDE	2360m
HEIGHT GAIN	1140m
AVERAGE GRADIENT	6%
TOUR DEBUT/CATEGORY	1922/HC

MAX GRADIENT 9%

18.9km

92 Col d'Agnel

The further south you travel through the Alps the more magnificent the climbs become and none more so than the Col d'Agnel – it is cycling paradise. You start the climb in the small town of Ville-Vieille, and then head south for 21 kilometres of sheer bliss, albeit extremely demanding sheer bliss. There's no consistency to the gradient to start with: small 10% ramps are hidden among the majority of 7%, climbing up to Molines-en-Queyras where you fork left following the signs to Italy. Pass through Pierre-Grosse, then Fontgillarde, up a fierce ramp and you enter stunning, pristine wilderness: bare slopes to your left, tree-covered to your right, and snow-capped peaks ahead. It's gentle at first but things soon turn nasty as the slope kicks up to 8 and then 9%; with seven tortuous kilometres still to ride you catch sight of the summit. Your surroundings are simply incredible – if your mouth weren't already locked open gulping in oxygen to feed your muscles, it would be gaping through sheer awe. The last 3 kilometres are brutal, so say goodbye to your saddle for the vicious fight to the peak where the climb ends on a knife-edge before plunging down into Italy.

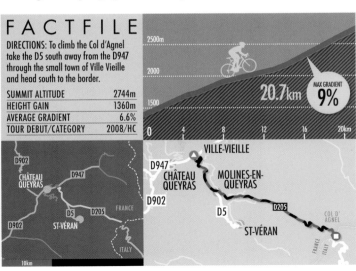

FACTFILE

DIRECTIONS: To climb the Col d'Agnel take the D5 south away from the D947 through the small town of Ville Vieille and head south to the border.

SUMMIT ALTITUDE	2744m
HEIGHT GAIN	1360m
AVERAGE GRADIENT	6.6%
TOUR DEBUT/CATEGORY	2008/HC

20.7km

MAX GRADIENT **9%**

VILLE-VIEILLE

D902

CHÂTEAU QUEYRAS

D947

D947

CHÂTEAU QUEYRAS

MOLINES-EN-QUEYRAS

D902

D5

D205

D5

D205

COL D' AGNEL

ST-VÉRAN

ST-VÉRAN

FRANCE

ITALY

FRANCE ITALY

10km

93 Col du Noyer

As soon as I arrived in this corner of France I loved it. I don't know exactly why, but it just seemed, well, perfect, and this, the Col du Noyer, is the perfect climb. Heading west from the N85, before you stands a foreboding rock face – an impassable ridge that dominates the skyline. For the first 8 kilometres you're riding towards it but not getting any closer, climbing ever so slightly but not getting any higher. It's not until you reach Noyer that things get interesting but boy is it worth the wait. As soon as you're away from the village, the gradient increases: 7% for the first kilometre then rising to 9% as the road weaves back and forth creeping up the ridge. After briefly falling back to 7%, the last 3 kilometres are a punishing 9% and it's time to tighten the straps as the tiny road – now clinging to the mountainside – heads to the summit. Framed by the sheer wall of rock to your right and the stunning view of the immense valley to your left, regardless of its severity, the road is a joy to ride. The final kilometre is packed with fabulous switchbacks stacked on top of each other, which deliver you to the summit on the grassy plateau in the shadow of jagged peaks on both sides.

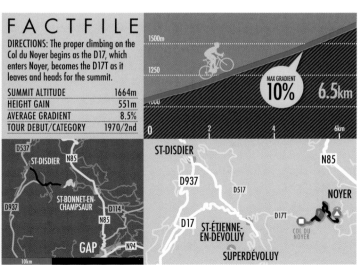

FACTFILE

DIRECTIONS: The proper climbing on the Col du Noyer begins as the D17, which enters Noyer, becomes the D17T as it leaves and heads for the summit.

SUMMIT ALTITUDE	1664m
HEIGHT GAIN	551m
AVERAGE GRADIENT	8.5%
TOUR DEBUT/CATEGORY	1970/2nd

MAX GRADIENT
10%   **6.5km**

1500m
1250
1000

0   2   4   6km

D537
ST-DISDIER   N85
D937
ST-BONNET-EN-CHAMPSAUR   D114
N85
GAP   N94
10km

ST-DISDIER
N85
D937
D517
NOYER
D17   D17T
ST-ÉTIENNE-EN-DEVOLUY   COL DU NOYER
SUPERDÉVOLUY

94 Col de Manse

There are a whole host of ways up and down this little climb that lies just to the north of Gap. This route heads north on the N85, which also forms the first half of the Col Bayard. It's hard up the first ramp, but within minutes you're free of town and heading round a 90-degree left-hand bend into the beautiful Provence countryside. Next you have a series of five hairpins mostly set on a mild 6% gradient with 1 kilometre of reasonably hard 8%. There's excellent provision for cyclists on the wide sweeping bends that lead you to the junction with the D944 where you turn right. The slope immediately eases back then levels a touch before it begins to climb once more, meandering leisurely through its quiet surroundings. Hovering around 7% for the last 3 kilometres, and a touch steeper for the finale as you round a bend, pass the Refuge Napoléon and the summit lies just ahead of you. Now with the climb completed, you can't leave this area without visiting the bend where Joseba Beloki crashed and Lance Armstrong 'cheated' and went off-road. The bend lies at the bottom end of the D314, marked with an 'X' on the map.

FACTFILE

DIRECTIONS: Starting on the N85, the Av. Commandant Dumont, head north away from the roundabout with the junction of the N94 in the north-east of Gap.

SUMMIT ALTITUDE	1278m
HEIGHT GAIN	530m
AVERAGE GRADIENT	5.9%
TOUR DEBUT/CATEGORY	1971/2nd

MAX GRADIENT
9%

1250m
1000
750
0   2   4   6   8km

9km

95 Col de Vars

I rode the Col de Vars on a blisteringly hot day; it was nudging 40 degrees in the valley and my tyres were sticking to the tarmac as I began climbing its exposed slopes. My skin crisping, mouth dry, hands welded to the lever hoods with a mixture of sweat and energy gel, there were moments when I really had to remind myself that I was having the time of my life. Riding the south side, I picked up the climb in Saint-Paul-sur-Ubaye, disregarding the gentle rise out of Les Gleizolles. It's not too tough to begin with: there's a slight excursion on to some 10% gradient, but for the most part, the first couple of kilometres are a more sedate 6%. There's a brief levelling when you reach Mélezen but after this it's hard, very hard. With 5 kilometres to go, it ramps up to 8%, and then into 2 kilometres of 10%, which slow all time and space. With a kilometre to go, after such a long time on this punishing gradient and in the searing heat, I entered a Zen-like state, my eyes fixed 3m in front of the bike. Pedal rev after pedal rev my task to reach the end transfixed me, then with 500m left, the slope finally backed off, and, released from its spell, I was able to click up from the 26 sprocket and attack the summit.

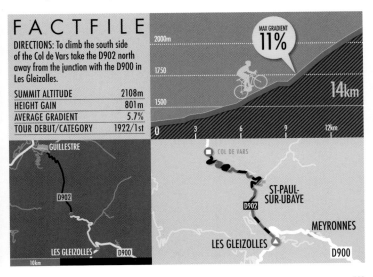

FACTFILE

DIRECTIONS: To climb the south side of the Col de Vars take the D902 north away from the junction with the D900 in Les Gleizolles.

SUMMIT ALTITUDE	2108m
HEIGHT GAIN	801m
AVERAGE GRADIENT	5.7%
TOUR DEBUT/CATEGORY	1922/1st

MAX GRADIENT **11%**

14km

2000m
1750
1500

0   3   6   9   12km

GUILLESTRE

D902

LES GLEIZOLLES   D900

10km

COL DE VARS

ST-PAUL-SUR-UBAYE

D902

MEYRONNES

LES GLEIZOLLES   D900

96 Pra Loup

The next stop on my out-of-season tour of French ski resorts brings me to Pra Loup, sitting high above Barcelonnette. Having never been skiing, I've never actually seen any of these hilltop outposts as they are meant to be seen; in the summer many simply lay abandoned – ghost towns in the clouds. Some, however, have adapted to the lack of snow, and in the warmer months become a haven for mountain bikers, climbers and others searching for a thrill, and Pra Loup is one of those. The climb has the same origins as both the Col d'Allos and the Col de la Cayolle. In the heart of Barcelonnette where you leave town on the D902, fork right at the junction on to the D908, and then, where signposted, join the D109. The next 5 kilometres of climbing, set between four majestic bends on a wide, ultra-smooth surface, you could ride all day long. It's the perfect training road: hard, up to 10% to test the legs, but only short so you never go too deeply into your reserves. Enter the first outpost, Pra Loup 1500, pass through, then make your way into the centre of town as the route becomes more and more congested to reach its peak at the back of the one-way circuit.

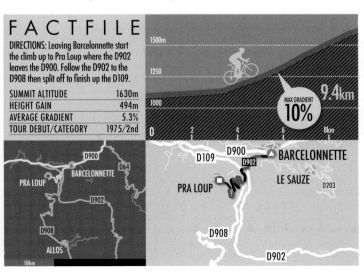

FACTFILE

DIRECTIONS: Leaving Barcelonnette start the climb up to Pra Loup where the D902 leaves the D900. Follow the D902 to the D908 then split off to finish up the D109.

SUMMIT ALTITUDE	1630m
HEIGHT GAIN	494m
AVERAGE GRADIENT	5.3%
TOUR DEBUT/CATEGORY	1975/2nd

MAX GRADIENT **10%**

9.4km

97 Col d'Allos

Two climbs leave Barcelonnette heading over the last of the Southern Alps: the Col de la Cayolle and the Col d'Allos. Both have Tour history, both are 17.5 kilometres long, but, having to ride just one, I went for the latter. Once free from town and past the turning to Pra Loup, the road immediately narrows and it's off into the wilderness. With the majority of its slopes set on a tame 5 to 6% gradient, and just a few patches of 8% and 10% mixed in to test the legs every now and again, it's not the toughest mountain you'll ride. What makes this road really special, though, is just how they managed to build it in the first place: it is a marvel of engineering. Twisting upwards, hugging the mountainside, teetering on the edge of oblivion, this tiny sliver of tarmac at times seems cut right out of the rock itself – round gullies, through knotted bends, it carves its path upwards. Not for the faint-hearted, the road feels hidden and is very quiet; it has a primeval charm, like riding through a land that time has forgotten. Higher up, however, the claustrophobia of the early slopes is replaced by open skies as you summit among the expansive rolling grassland that lies nestled beneath jagged peaks.

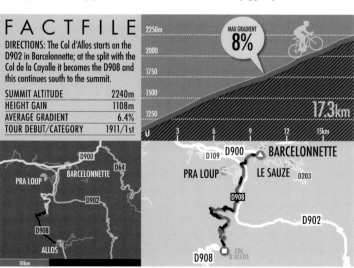

FACTFILE

DIRECTIONS: The Col d'Allos starts on the D902 in Barcelonnette; at the split with the Col de la Cayolle it becomes the D908 and this continues south to the summit.

SUMMIT ALTITUDE	2240m
HEIGHT GAIN	1108m
AVERAGE GRADIENT	6.4%
TOUR DEBUT/CATEGORY	1911/1st

MAX GRADIENT
8%

17.3km

98 Cime de la Bonette

There is a word that's used far too often today – one that's attributed to just about anything cycling related – but in this book I'm going to use it just the once, so here goes: the Cime de la Bonette is – EPIC. In 23 kilometres you'll climb up to 2,802m to a place where only the toughest of plants survive, high enough to touch the sky. On leaving Jausiers, the early slopes are a comfortable 6 to 7%, and predominantly straight, with a few clusters of hairpins thrown in. Reach halfway and there's a slight dip where you can shake the legs; freshen them here, because the second half is a tougher prospect set on 8 to 9% slopes. The higher you climb, the wilder things become. The grandeur of your surroundings increases exponentially as you twist your way through the boulder-strewn landscape. It is coarse, unspoiled, prehistoric. How they managed to plot a road through this inhospitable scenery is a wonder, but they did, and, as usual, it is perfectly smooth. Higher and higher you climb, past the point where not even grass will grow, to reach the Col de Bonette at 2,715m, but that's not the top. In front of you lies the Cime de la Bonette, the hostile, cruel finale, a wickedly steep loop purposely constructed to claim the title of highest road in France.

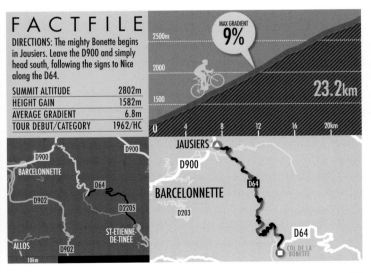

FACTFILE

DIRECTIONS: The mighty Bonette begins in Jausiers. Leave the D900 and simply head south, following the signs to Nice along the D64.

SUMMIT ALTITUDE	2802m
HEIGHT GAIN	1582m
AVERAGE GRADIENT	6.8m
TOUR DEBUT/CATEGORY	1962/HC

MAX GRADIENT
9%

23.2km

JAUSIERS
D900

BARCELONNETTE
D203

D64

COL DE LA BONETTE

D900
BARCELONNETTE
D64
D902
D2205
ST-ETIENNE-DE-TINEE
ALLOS
D902
10km

99 Col de la Lombarde

Whilst traversing the Alps having just conquered the Col de Bonette, anyone in their right mind will now be enjoying the 100 kilometre descent to the warm waters of the Côte d'Azur. But in my book, to bypass the Col de la Lombarde is a crime, because you really miss a treat. Leaving the tiny town of Isola, the first 3 kilometres are set on a vicious 9% before it settles down to a more sedate 6%. Packed with tangled hairpins, you cross back and forth over the river, tracking its course skyward. At halfway, the road eases back and it feels comparatively flat, but be assured, you're still rising and it steps up sharply on the approach to the resort of Isola 2000. Tour stages have finished here a couple of times, but you need to push on through to the edge of town, where – BOOM! What come next are 500m of the toughest climbing I have found in the Southern Alps. They destroy your rhythm, and push you into the red to have the legs and lungs screaming. And unfortunately, things don't get much easier. On paper it doesn't look this hard but I really struggled through these last 4 kilometres, the unusually red rocks surrounding me, to slump over my bars at the tiny summit and the border with Italy.

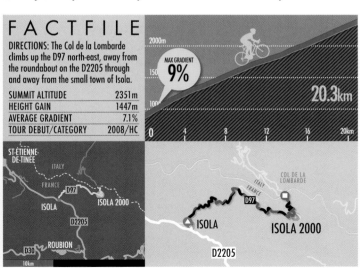

FACTFILE

DIRECTIONS: The Col de la Lombarde climbs up the D97 north-east, away from the roundabout on the D2205 through and away from the small town of Isola.

SUMMIT ALTITUDE	2351m
HEIGHT GAIN	1447m
AVERAGE GRADIENT	7.1%
TOUR DEBUT/CATEGORY	2008/HC

MAX GRADIENT
9%

20.3km

100 Mont Ventoux

There is no more formidable sight in the whole of cycling than that of Mont Ventoux as it appears on the horizon. To say it dominates the scenery is an understatement matched in magnitude only by the shivers it sends down your spine. If you only ever ride one mountain, make sure it's this one: brutal on the body, oozing history, and set in the most stunning scenery in France – if not the world. There are three ways to the top and the classic route is to head east from Bédoin via Chalet-Reynard; the first 3 kilometres are gentle but the giant looms over your left shoulder, and with 15 kilometres to go you turn to face it. Round the first hairpin the gradient rises and rises, twisting and turning at times on a camber so severe it resembles a bobsleigh track running through the craggy landscape. At Chalet-Reynard you leave the forest to face the infamous mistral wind, which even on a mild day has the power to bring you to a dead stop, but at least it helps dry the sweat from your handlebars. The final journey to the summit, across the desolate peak, is without doubt the most unique and wonderful experience you can have on two wheels, which, together with the satisfaction of reaching the top, makes Ventoux THE greatest cycling climb in France.

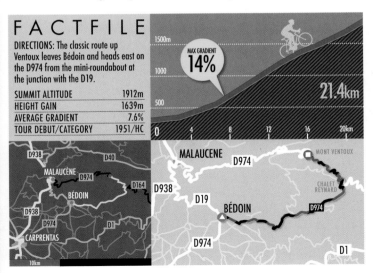

FACTFILE

DIRECTIONS: The classic route up Ventoux leaves Bédoin and heads east on the D974 from the mini-roundabout at the junction with the D19.

SUMMIT ALTITUDE	1912m
HEIGHT GAIN	1639m
AVERAGE GRADIENT	7.6%
TOUR DEBUT/CATEGORY	1951/HC

MAX GRADIENT **14%**

21.4km

1500m
1000
500
0   4   8   12   16   20km

D938 D40
MALAUCÈNE D974
D164
BÉDOIN
D938
D974 D1
CARPRENTAS

10km

MALAUCENE D974 MONT VENTOUX
D938
D19 CHALET REYNARD
BÉDOIN D974
D974 D1

So you want to be a climber

Well, tick this lot off and you'll be well on your way. Of course we're not all born to fly up mountains like Federico Bahamontes, but the more you practise, the better you get – or at least you'll lose some weight, which will help tip things in your favour. Now, it's quite an undertaking, both logistically and physically to ride all these climbs, especially in one summer, but it's not impossible. I'll leave that up to you. Once you have, though, or have even just ridden a few, each year when the Tour de France is on TV you can turn to your friends and family and say, 'I rode up there!'

No	Climb	Date ridden	Direction	Time
	PYRENEES			
1	Port de Larrau			
2	Col du Soudet			
3	Col de Marie-Blanque			
4	Col d'Aubisque			
5	Col du Soulor			
6	Hautacam			
7	Luz Ardiden			
8	Col du Tourmalet			
9	Col d'Aspin			
10	Pla d'Adet			
11	Col d'Azet			
12	Col de Peyresourde			
13	Port de Balès			
14	Superbagnères			
15	Col du Portillon			
16	Col de Menté			
17	Col des Ares			
18	Col de Portet-d'Aspet			
19	Col de la Core			
20	Guzet-Neige			

No	Climb	Date ridden	Direction	Time
21	Col de Latrape			
22	Col d'Agnes			
23	Port de Lers			
24	Mur de Péguère			
25	Col de Port			
26	Plateau de Beille			
27	Ax 3 Domaines			
28	Port de Pailhères			
29	Col d'Ordino			
30	Andorre-Arcalís			

MASSIF CENTRAL				
No	Climb	Date ridden	Direction	Time
31	Col de Vendeix			
32	Col de la Croix Saint-Robert			
33	Col de la Croix Morand			
34	Super-Besse			
35	Col des Pradeaux			
36	Col de la Croix-de-l'Homme Mort			
37	Col de la République			
38	Col de la Croix-de-Chaubouret			
39	Col de l'Oeillon			
40	Col d'Entremont			
41	Col de Prat de Bouc			
42	Pas de Peyrol			
43	Côte de la Croix-Neuve			

VOSGES				
No	Climb	Date ridden	Direction	Time
44	Col du Donon			
45	Col du Calvaire			

No	Climb	Date ridden	Direction	Time
46	Collet du Linge			
47	Col de la Schlucht			
48	Col du Firstplan			
49	Col du Platzerwasel			
50	Grand Ballon			
51	Ballon d'Alsace			
52	Ballon de Servance			
53	Planche des Belles Filles			

JURA				
No	Climb	Date ridden	Direction	Time
54	Côte des Rousses			
55	Col de la Faucille			
56	Col de la Croix de la Serra			
57	Col du Berthiand			
58	Col du Grand Colombier			
59	Mont du Chat			

ALPES DU NORD				
No	Climb	Date ridden	Direction	Time
60	Col du Corbier			
61	Avoriaz			
62	Col de Joux Plane			
63	Col de la Colombière			
64	Semnoz			
65	Col de la Croix-Fry			
66	Col des Aravis			
67	Col des Saisies			
68	Cormet de Roseland			
69	Col du Petit-Saint-Bernard			
70	Col de Tamié			
71	Col du Grand Cucheron			

No	Climb	Date ridden	Direction	Time
72	Col du Granier			
73	Col du Cucheron			
74	Col de Porte			
75	Col de la Madeleine			
76	Courchevel			
77	La Plagne			
78	Col de l'Iseran			
79	Col du Mont-Cenis			
80	La Toussuire			
81	Col du Glandon			
82	Col de la Croix de Fer			
83	Alpe d'Huez			
84	Col d'Ornon			
85	Les Deux Alpes			
86	Col du Télégraphe			
87	Col du Galibier			

ALPES DU SUD				
No	Climb	Date ridden	Direction	Time
88	Col du Lautaret			
89	Col du Granon			
90	Sestrieres			
91	Col d'Izoard			
92	Col d'Agnel			
93	Col du Noyer			
94	Col de Manse			
95	Col de Vars			
96	Pra Loup			
97	Col d'Allos			
98	Cime de la Bonette			
99	Col de la Lombarde			
100	Mont Ventoux			

Thank You

Thanks firstly to my wife Charlotte for again accommodating my self-indulgent hobby and, of course, to my amazing kids for 'enjoying the views' as we crossed the Alps after Daddy confiscated the DVD player. Of course I couldn't drag the family on all five research trips, so for their sanity and mine I employed the services of three additional travelling companions. Big thanks go to Owen Cooper, a new recruit to cycling who well and truly found his mountain legs after chasing the Tour for five days around the Alps. Next to Nick Burton for his excellent company as we discovered the Massif Central, followed by a pilgrimage to Ventoux for one of the best days on a bike either of us have ever had. Then, thirdly, to my dad – together we shared ten days of mountains, vultures, and three-course dinners while crossing the Pyrenees on an adventure I will treasure forever. Of course, thanks also to their wives for allowing them to come out and play, and thanks to my mum and mother-in-law Gill for helping hold the fort while I was away.

Other people who've played a key part in the success of this project and whom I'd like to thank are Richard Wood at Extra UK, Tim Bayley at Fisher Outdoor Leisure, and Mike Hawkins at Cycling Weekly. Thanks to everyone at the Cycle Show, especially Graham Little, Magnus Backstedt, and the Downing brothers, who made me feel at ease in a very unfamiliar environment.

A massive thanks to Nick Andrews, Katy Trevethan, and Anita Rani at the BBC for an amazing couple of days filming in the Scottish Highlands, and to Allen Bridge for hosting the launch party for my third book, *Hellingen*. Thanks also to Andy Waterman, Jason Humphries, Gordon Knight, Simon Hursthouse, Luke Evans, Simon Richardson, Pete Muir, and, of course, everyone who buys the books and follows my adventures on Twitter.

I couldn't have completed this project without cross-referencing some existing material, especially Chris Sidwell's *Tour Climbs*, *Mountain High* by Daniel Friebe and Pete Goding, and back issues of cycling magazines. On the internet, several sites proved invaluable: *Climbbybike* and *Ledicodutour*, and thirdly *Strava* for double-checking start and finish points and for pushing me to foolishly try to record my best time up each mountain. Finally I'd like to thank the road builders of France for laying some of the smoothest, fault-free stretches of tarmac over some of the most inhospitable and inaccessible parts of their beautiful nation: they are masters of their craft, so again, *chapeau*.